The Times Opera Notes

For Anna

"Eating, loving, singing and digesting are, in truth,
the four acts of the comic opera known as life,
and they pass like the bubbles of a bottle of champagne.
Whoever lets them break without having enjoyed them
is a fool."

Gioachino Rossini

THE TIMES

OPERA NOTES

Robert Thicknesse

HarperCollins*Publishers*
77–85 Fulham Palace Road
Hammersmith
London W6 8JB

www.collins.co.uk

First published in 2001 by HarperCollins*Publishers*
This edition published 2007

Reprint 10 9 8 7 6 5 4 3 2

ISBN 978–0–00–725467–5

The Times is a registered trademark of Times Newspapers Ltd

British Library Cataloguing in Publication Data
A catalogue record for this book is available from
the British Library

Typeset in Great Britain by
Davidson Pre-Press Graphics Ltd, Glasgow G3

Printed and bound in Great Britain by
Clays Ltd, St Ives plc.

CONTENTS

Introduction   7

Introduction

To say that opera is the most life-affirming of the arts may seem a curious statement, considering its immense death-toll. Its personnel are embodiments of human weaknesses, which coincidentally double as their greatest strengths. Their grandiose efforts to reach for the stars always end in disaster; their obsession with honour inevitably results in their deaths; they are, unlike the audience (one hopes) indifferent – when not actively hostile – to the bonds of matrimony. They are volcanoes of hysteria, neurosis, ambition and raging adolescent hormones. If their world is not godless, this impious bunch expend considerable energy in contravening the strictures of religion and the norms of civilised behaviour. Yet opera contains two great lessons: that it is good to be alive, and that there are worse things than death.

There is good *prima facie* evidence to support the frequently mooted idea that opera is a dead art form. Of the 90-odd operas in this book, which reflects the core repertoire as found in any of the world's major opera houses, all but 18 were composed in fewer than 150 years between 1781, the year of Mozart's first featured work, *Idomeneo*, and 1926, that of *Turandot*, Puccini's last. The most recent is Poulenc's *Dialogues des Carmélites* of 1956, and no living composers appear.

Nonetheless, the contemporary operatic scene is thriving for the first time since the early 20th century, nowhere more so than in staid old England, where it seems that to criminalise attendance at or participation in opera is the dear wish of many (perhaps to be accomplished when those pesky smokers have finally been hounded to extinction). In 2004, Covent Garden was full for the première run of Thomas Adès's *The Tempest*: not yet a repertory work, but in 20 years it may well be. It takes a long time for operas to become accepted into the repertoire: 20 years ago a book like this would not have contained the operas of Britten, Janáček or Poulenc; nor, for that matter, anything of Handel beyond *Julius Caesar*. It is a fair bet that within a generation, as well as Turnage, the operas of Thomas Adès, Gian Carlo Menotti, Peter Maxwell Davies, Harrison Birtwistle, Leonard Bernstein, John Adams, Sergei Prokofiev and Michael Tippett will be as frequently performed as those of Britten are now – and, no doubt, Vivaldi, Lully and Rameau will be as common as Handel.

It is a little over 400 years since the birth of opera. It is characteristic for there to be some confusion about what exactly opera is for, and this is evident at the outset when in the 1580s the group of Florentine intellectuals known as the Camerata conceived a mixture of music and theatre along the lines of Greek drama – the point being that they had no idea actually what

Greek drama sounded or looked like. As so often in the subsequent history of music, what they were doing was a reaction against current trends, namely both the inadequacy of polyphonic music – a more or less ornate, multi-part idiom, usually written for a church choir – to convey the meaning of words, and the over-ornateness of madrigals, which had developed a highly expressive musical language to do just that.

What the members of the Camerata – notably Vincenzo Galilei, Galileo's father – proposed was a drama featuring a single vocal strand (the "monodic line") which would reproduce the rhythms of natural speech and highlight the words: in later times this, or something like it, would become known as recitative. The effect would be of a simply sung or declaimed play. The history of opera is a cycle of the corruption of this ideal by an ever-greater emphasis on purely musical and vocal beauty – 18th-century *opera seria*, the *bel canto* of Bellini and Donizetti – and the inevitable attempt to revert to a version of first principles – for example in the work of Gluck, Wagner, and to an extent Musorgsky, Janáček and much 20th-century opera.

There were operatic composers before Monteverdi, and he wrote several before *L'Incoronazione di Poppea* (1643), the earliest opera to feature in this book, but it is a good place to start because it blends the ideals of the Camerata, albeit somewhat diluted by this stage, with opera's greatest obsession, sex. The monodic line is there, but it is mixed in with madrigals and the embryonic form of the aria, a musical soliloquy which was soon to become a vocal showpiece in which the words would assume ever lesser significance. *Poppea* is already much more "tuneful" than the Camerata would have liked, and even the linking recitatives have acquired a *continuo* accompaniment: keyboard, viola da gamba, lutes.

In the second half of the 17th century opera developed along national lines. In Italy this consisted of a growing distinction between recitative and aria, in France the regrettable synthesis whereby "the characters' entire happiness and entire sorrow consists of watching people dance around them", and in England an evolution of the traditional form of the masque, which alternated spoken episodes with musical interludes, as in Purcell's *Fairy Queen*, based on *A Midsummer Night's Dream*. The little miracle of *Dido and Aeneas*, which might have formed the basis of a truly English operatic tradition, seems to have come and gone without anyone noticing.

The 18th century was dominated by singers, particularly the infamous castrati, whose combination of power, amazing vocal agility and an unearthly purity of tone – not to mention *prima donna* tendencies – contributed hugely to the success of *opera seria*. Largely drawn from classical mythology, *opere serie* were morality plays for European potentates, though whether they had any effect is open to question. Drama was a secondary consideration in these costume concerts: the stagings were largely static and the only reason anyone went was to hear the vocal dynamite of the singers and catch the latest developments in theatrical machinery. *Opera seria* introduced the curious notion of the "exit aria", which involves the singer leaving the stage at the end simply in order to be able to return to collect applause. Handel's operas are easily the finest examples of *opera seria*, and somewhat exempt from these criticisms: the most theatrical of composers, he epitomised the Baroque in the way he stretched boundaries while contriving to work within existing conventions.

Gluck was opera's first great reformer, and reverted to an understated style of pure classicism without vocal exhibitionism, where the words could reassert supremacy. His famous manifesto stated his intention "to eliminate all those abuses which had been introduced to Italian Opera partly through the ill-advised vanity of singers and partly through the excessive complaisance of composers". If nobody actually followed his lead, he at least dealt a death-blow to *opera seria* and established the conditions for Mozart's operas to be written. Mozart composed operas in all the existing traditions: *opera seria*, Neapolitan *buffa* – a form of comic drama dreamt up by playwright Carlo Goldoni and set to music by the likes of Paisiello and Cimarosa – and *Singspiel*, the nascent German form with embarrassing spoken dialogue. Mozart's revolution lay in making the music itself the prime mover of drama and character, indivisible from the words. In this he was greatly helped by having his best librettos written by the reprobate Lorenzo da Ponte, a man who understood that the words of an opera must leave room for the music.

After Mozart, opera again began to fragment. The German *Singspiel* developed through Beethoven and Weber to early Wagner (and, *mutatis mutandis*, into the romantic operas of other European countries, notably Bohemia); the French took off in another direction with "Grand Opera", a form in which spectacle and massive set-pieces were the thing. It also became obligatory to include a ballet during the course of Act II to satisfy the young bloods of the Jockey Club, who would pile into the Paris Opéra after dinner to ogle the dancers and plan their after-show assignations. Anyone who ignored this unwritten rule was in for trouble: inevitably, it was Wagner who copped it, when the 1871 première of the Paris version of *Tannhäuser* was whistled off stage. *Opera buffa* was taken in hand by Rossini, who invented the style known as *bel canto* – lots of vocal show-offery – and also laid the foundations of the formal structures that Italian opera would adhere to for the next generation and more. This is often known as the "cabaletta style", after the generally gymnastic final section of an aria, and was a flexible means of building excitement over extended periods. The influence of this system can be seen even in such un-Rossinian productions as *Tannhäuser*, but is met mostly in the works of Rossini's successors, Donizetti, Bellini and Verdi, who developed a line of romantic opera – comic and tragic – culminating in the bloodbaths of *Il Trovatore*, *Don Carlos* and *La Forza del Destino*.

Most of the later 19th century looks like a straight dust-up between Verdi and Wagner. Much of Verdi's early work was written in a muscular version of *bel canto*, but by the end of his life he had done away with the old "numbers" that made up all operas to this point, and by the time of *Otello* and *Falstaff* was writing operas of virtually continuous music, the distinction between aria and recitative dissolved to a point where the terms lose their meaning. Wagner was doing the same, naturally in a very different way. In his later works, *The Ring*, *Tristan and Isolde* and *Parsifal*, he attempted to compose what he called *Gesamtkunstwerke*, unified works of art where words, music, drama and staging combined seamlessly into an entirely new art-form: the old Greek ideal again, in fact.

The basis of this is Wagner's system of *leitmotive*, literally "leading motifs": every character, mood, action and thing has its own musical motto. In Wagner's imitators this can be an irritatingly parrot-like habit, but the man's extraordinary architectural imagination, allied to an ability to do things with the orchestra that nobody had dreamed of before, created many-layered effects of huge complexity and stunning effect. It is not uncommon to hear complaints about the lack of tunes in Wagner, but this misses the point (and is also untrue). Expression purely through melody was not his thing: *everything* contributes. The intellectual achievement of his works is incomprehensibly great, and if you occasionally hear what sounds like a wrong note – unlike in Mozart, for example – you can bet there are nine or ten good reasons why that note could not possibly be any other note. Unwilling to be associated with the fripperies of Italian opera, Wagner denied that operas were what he wrote: *Parsifal* was a *Bühnenweihfestspiel*, or "stage-consecration-festival-play".

Wagner's influence was huge and inescapable, even affecting such a wildly different composer as Puccini. One of the great populists, Puccini combined highly effective music with tear-jerking drama to create what most people probably still think of as the *ne plus ultra* of opera, but highbrows have always been a bit sniffy about him. When Britten told Shostakovich he thought Puccini wrote "dreadful" operas, the Russian got closer to the truth when he replied: "No, Ben, you are wrong. He writes dreadful music, but *wonderful* operas." Actually, quite a lot of Puccini's *music* is pretty good, too.

Wagner had taken music to the edge of apparent breakdown, and the diatonic system, based on the tension between major and minor moods, which had been flexible enough to accommodate the previous 500 years' music, seemed on the brink of collapse. Debussy and Berg, in opera as well as their other works, experimented beyond its boundaries, but opera is essentially a conservative medium, which is why *Pelléas and Mélisande* and *Wozzeck* are still in many ways the most "modern-sounding" works in this book. Twentieth-century opera is a story of composers rather than schools or styles. Richard Strauss surpassed even Wagner in staggering romanticism. Janáček and Britten, the other indisputable colossi of the century, wrote psychodramas of great power, in entirely original musical idioms. Gershwin and Bernstein factored in American music. Stravinsky (in *The Rake's Progress*) and Poulenc returned to neo-classical roots with different aims and results. Modern times have been dominated by the "minimalists" – Philip Glass, John Adams (*Nixon in China*), Michael Nyman – specialising in a kind of hypnotic, repeating, often electronic music, often of great beauty and power. Harrison Birtwistle carries the torch for modernism. The other composers mentioned at the beginning might be described as hybrids, seeking to reinvent opera and music theatre as a kind of synthesis of 20th-century styles. Where this is leading is far from clear.

This book aims to perform a modest service: most opera-goers are content to spend their lives in a state of mild bafflement concerning the finer points of operatic plot and motivation, a situation aggravated by the wilfully over-complicated nature of most programme synopses. One aim, therefore, is, in the words of the helpful librettist of Cavalli's *Veremonda*, to provide "*a Summary of the Opera for those who cannot understand it having heard & read the Same*". Opera should be celebrated for its absurdity as much as for anything else. Plots are often of minor importance, but this is no reason not to laugh at them. And while you may think that the *Crush Bar gambits* in the following pages are extreme or perverse, some director somewhere (probably a German) has placed even more bizarre interpretations on these works. Dates given are those of first performances.

The object is to entertain, and to give some modest idea of what makes these operas special: in its own way each is a high-point of human achievement. But there is more than one way of enjoying opera. If this book raises a laugh, encourages an interest in this most approachable of art forms, or even brings a wan smile to the lips of jaded *aficionados*, it will have served its purpose.

Adriana Lecouvreur

FRANCESCO CILEA (1902)

Snuffed out – with a sniff!

In short: A French tragedienne drops down dead upon receiving a proposal of marriage from an illegitimate German pretender to the Polish throne.

MUSIC

An undeservedly obscure opera – a sort of polite Puccini – which always knows exactly the right moves to make. Despite being extremely easy to listen to, and despite the slick use of operatic conventions, there is nothing facile about it: at its best it has a dignity often lacking in Puccini; it is beautifully scored, it rises to very effective romantic climaxes, and the more obvious sentimentality is offset by witty ensembles and characters of more than melodramatic interest. The chatty theatricals owe plenty to Verdi's *Falstaff* and had an effect on Puccini's one-act knockabout *Gianni Schicchi*. A favourite vehicle for your more mature *prima donna*.

WORDS

A plot of almost complete incomprehensibility, thanks to some inept cutting by librettist Arturo Colautti of Eugène Scribe's play.

PLOT

Act I 1730. *Adriana, star turn at the Comédie Française, waits with bated breath for a post-show date with Maurizio, an ambitious German-born French general, but he blows her out in order to meet the Princess of Bouillon, whom he hopes will further his cause. Her husband, thinking Maurizio is arranging a tryst with his own mistress (another actress), arranges a surprise party at the same address.*

Act II *The Princess turns out to be after more than political discussions, and wigs out with jealousy when Maurizio gives her the brush-off – plus a bunch of* *violets that Adriana gave him earlier that evening. The Prince (plus guests) arrives, and much confusion follows before Adriana (remarkably, taking Maurizio's word that nothing fishy has been going on) helps the Princess to get away unnoticed. Thanks to the dark, neither recognises the other, but they still manage to have a catfight re Maurizio.*

Act III *At a subsequent bash at the Bouillons the penny drops for the Princess and Adriana, who is invited to do a party-piece and chooses an obscure monologue about adultery which she addresses meaningfully to the Princess, driving her crazy.*

Act IV *Adriana is in a decline: she has retired from the stage and Maurizio seems to be off the scene. Her colleagues come to cheer her up and she also receives a bunch of flowers – "from Maurizio" – which is of course that old posy of violets, sent by the Princess. She takes a whiff. Poison! But before she dies she has time to effect a reconciliation with Maurizio, get engaged and have a miniature mad scene.*

Don't ask

Er, did something happen between Acts III and IV that they forgot to tell us about?

Fancy that

The real Adrienne Lecouvreur actually managed to survive a poisoned-chockie assassination attempt and finally died of dysentery in the arms of Voltaire (yuck!).

Crush Bar gambit

"*Adriana* is a study of a curious dissociative disorder endemic in the acting profession. Imprisoned by vanity in her identification with the fated heroines of Greek tragedy, but with a personal life closer to Feydeau farce, Adriana avidly pursues an entirely avoidable destiny. Cause of death is perceived dramatic imperative, and obviously not the physically impossible poisoned violets."

Recordings

❖ Capuana, Tebaldi, Simionato, del Monaco, Fioravanti, St Cecilia Rome Academy Chorus and Orchestra (Decca) ❖ Levine, Scotto, Domingo, Milnes, Obraztsova, Ambrosian Opera Chorus, Philharmonia Orchestra (CBS) ❖

Aida

GIUSEPPE VERDI (1871)

Walling-in, Memphis!

In short: *An Egyptian general avoids marrying the woman he doesn't love by getting buried alive instead.*

MUSIC

Composed neither for the opening of the Suez Canal nor of the Cairo Opera House, though it was first performed there after an eleven-month delay caused when the scenery failed to arrive from Paris owing to the small matter of a Prussian siege. Known (and generally loved) for its visual and aural spectacle, Verdi's grandest opera is also one of his most surprisingly intimate, centred on three rather confused people and their incompatible desires, and culminating in his most rapt ending. Delicate scene-painting (the nocturnal Act III oasis), modal exotica (the eerie harp-backed temple invocations), muscular hymns (*Su del Nilo*), grand marches and emotional ensembles combine with the simplest and most vulnerable love-arias (*Celeste Aida* and *O cieli azzurri* with its tremolo violins and oboe curlicues) in the greatest all-rounder in the repertoire.

WORDS

A translation by Antonio Ghislanzoni of a work by the Egyptologist Auguste Mariette, the subject of which he apparently borrowed from his brother's projected novel without asking. Both Verdi and Camille du Locle, librettist of *Don Carlos*, had a sizeable hand in it too.

PLOT

Act I *Radames, divinely appointed C-in-C of the Egyptian army, is in a bit of a corner: the pharaoh's daughter Amneris is in love with him but he has eyes only for her slave, the Ethiopian Aida. The latter, too, is not sure which side to support in the forthcoming Egypt-Ethiopia match, particularly since her father is the Ethiopian king (though nobody else knows this).*

Act II *Radames and his lads whip the Ethiopians. Amneris has noticed the way Radames and Aida keep looking at each other and is none too happy. The king frees the Ethiopian prisoners, which is unpopular with the clergy, only keeping Aida's father Amonasro as a hostage. Then he suggests that Radames and Amneris should get married.*

Act III *Amonasro wonders whether Aida can't find out from Radames the proposed invasion route the Egyptians will be taking in their retaliatory strike against Ethiopia. She feels rotten about this, but tries anyway, and Radames tells her. He is immediately arrested for treason.*

Act IV *Amneris tries to get Radames off the hook but fails. He is buried alive, but his day, which seems to be heading downhill fast, brightens up a bit when he finds that Aida has managed to sneak into his tomb.*

WHAT THE CRITICS SAID
"An obsequious imitation of Wagner." (Pietro Cominazzi; actually Verdi didn't hear a Wagner opera until after he'd composed it.)

STRANGE BUT TRUE
The big Act II hymn *Gloria all'Egitto* nearly became the Egyptian national anthem (but the Khedive was overruled by the Ottomans).

FANCY THAT
During a run in Padua in 1872 the backstage bar had to be nailed shut after the chorus kept turning up "abominably drunk".

CRUSH BAR GAMBIT
"This amazingly prescient story of a clerico-fascist state's invasion of Ethiopia was clearly inspired by Verdi's fears about the new Italy's expansionist and totalitarian tendencies, raised by its opportunistic seizing of Rome (defended by dejected French troops) during the Franco-Prussian war."

RECORDINGS
❖ Karajan, Tebaldi, Bergonzi, Simoniato, MacNeil, Vienna Singverein, Vienna Philharmonic (Decca) ❖ Karajan, Freni, Carreras, Baltsa, Cappuccilli, Vienna State Opera Chorus, Vienna Philharmonic (EMI) ❖

Alcina

GEORGE FRIDERIC HANDEL (1735)

She turned men into beasts!

In short: *A nymphomaniac enchantress loses her charms.*

MUSIC

Naughtily turns the Enlightenment sentiments of the libretto on their heads: the words say reason is better than passion but the music begs to differ. Handel had learned something worthwhile about English taste from John Gay's mickey-taking *Beggar's Opera* and *Alcina* is notably more dramatic than your average *opera seria*. The characters, too, have much more individual music than usual: Alcina's drips with languid eroticism, something of a contrast to the butch Bradamante which makes you think Ruggiero might have a better time staying put. Add a refreshingly amoral sex-kitten for Alcina's sister Morgana and a handful of jaunty ballets and rousing choruses for an unmissable show. Top numbers: Ruggiero's *Verdi prati*, one of those wistful minuettish airs Handel pulls out of the hat apparently at will, and Alcina's *Ah! cor mio*, the height of sensuality, all droopy appoggiaturas over plucked strings.

WORDS

A largely irrelevant and thoroughly silly episode from Ariosto's epic 16th-century poem *Orlando Furioso*, which catalogues the adventures of Roland, Charlemagne's right-hand man, and his pals – with a few Arthurian legends thrown in for good measure.

PLOT

Act I *Ruggiero (formerly a castrato but now a mezzo) has been ensnared by the sexy Alcina; his girlfriend Bradamante comes to fetch him home disguised as her own brother Ricciardo. Ruggiero fails to recognise her. Alcina's sister Morgana (a guest appearance by Morgan le Fay) falls in love with Ricciardo/Bradamante, annoying her own boyfriend Oronte, who decides to make trouble by telling Ruggiero that Alcina is in love with Ricciardo.*

Act II *Ruggiero – in common with the audience – is thoroughly confused (but still in love with Alcina). After a talking-to from a man purporting to be his old tutor he realises his behaviour has fallen short of 18th-century ideals and decides to be in love with Bradamante (whom he finally recognises) again. He plans his escape.*

Act III *Ruggiero and Bradamante see off Alcina's soldiers, and, before they leave, release all Alcina's ex-lovers from the various spells which had turned them into rocks, bushes, etc.*

DON'T ASK
Just why Bradamante thinks dressing up as her brother is a good idea, when it is obviously bound to cause considerable trouble.

STRANGE BUT TRUE
Handel's first Ruggiero, the drippy castrato Carestini, refused to sing *Verdi prati* because it was too dull. After initial success, *Alcina* wasn't performed between 1737 and 1957, when Richard Bonynge and Joan Sutherland resurrected it.

CRUSH BAR GAMBIT
"*Alcina* is the epitome of opera as runaway id: a catalogue of unrestrained sexual fantasy encompassing virtually every gender permutation – a *Rocky Horror Show* for the 1730s. Eunuchs in love with women, women falling for other women in drag, men of ambiguous masculinity going for women of dubious sexuality. Handel's credentials as a proto-Jungian are thoroughly vindicated by his choice of the archetype of schoolmaster to represent the deadening hand of the super-ego."

RECORDINGS
❖ Bonynge, Sutherland, Sinclair, Berganza, Freni, London Symphony Orchestra (Decca: a gloriously inauthentic performance) ❖ Hickox, Augér, Jones, Kuhlmann, Harrhy, City of London Baroque Sinfonia, Opera Stage Chorus (EMI) ❖

Andrea Chénier

UMBERTO GIORDANO (1896)

Upstarts downstairs!

In short: *An aristocratic young woman takes a few with her when nabbed by revolutionaries.*

MUSIC

A busy score, flitting from theme to theme and key to key, full of burgeoning violin tunes, thoroughly competent and undemanding, like a top-dollar film score. If it doesn't reach sustained heights, it is never less than pleasant, from the *Bohème*-like bustling opening to the final moments of passion as André and Madeleine trundle off to their doom in nice Mr Sanson's tumbrel. The mood-music is really well done, by turns elegiac, ethereal, gloomy and lyrical. Gérard is an unusually interesting character, torn between politics, his feelings for Madeleine, and a certain ambiguous attitude towards his former employers.

WORDS

An original libretto by Luigi Illica, written for the kind-hearted Baron Franchetti – the fellow Puccini tricked out of the *Tosca* libretto – who gave it to the impoverished Giordano.

PLOT

Act I A party thrown by the Countess of Coigny in Paris in 1786 is ruined by bolshy butler Gérard, who amusingly smuggles in a load of down-and-outs before handing in his cards. Among those present are revolutionary poet André Chénier and the countess's daughter, Madeleine, who teases him.

Act II *Three years later, and Chénier has been receiving anonymous* billets doux. *His friend Roucher tells him to forget it, they are obviously from a complete tart, and he'd do better to clear out of the country. Actually, of course, they are from Madeleine, who arranges a rendezvous with Chénier, in the course of which they decide they are in love. Sadly Chénier is being followed on the orders of Gérard, now a big-shot in the Revolution, who wants to get his hands (literally) on Madeleine. He and Chénier have a fight while Madeleine escapes. Gérard is wounded and in an access of nobility refuses to divulge his opponent's name.*

Act III *Chénier has now been arrested and is being used as bait to trap Madeleine. It works: she shows up at Gérard's office to try to rescue him (price, ça va sans dire, her virtue). However after she tells Gérard her sob-story he has a change of heart and vows to get Chénier off the hook. But it's a bit late: Chénier is tried, rudimentarily, and sentenced to death.*

Act IV *Madeleine substitutes herself for a female prisoner and in a heartwarming scene she and Chénier set off for the guillotine together.*

STRANGE BUT TRUE
Giordano wrote most of the opera in a undertaker's shop surrounded by corpses, the only place he could afford in Milan. His second-most-famous composition is probably the jingle he wrote for Italian radio news.

CRUSH BAR GAMBIT
"Madeleine is obviously playing a long game here, and takes elaborate revenge on the class enemies responsible for the destruction of her world: the treacherous poet Chénier with his inflammatory verses, the butler Gérard, whose passion for her is perverted by social envy into empty revolutionary fervour, and her own maid Bersi, whom she vindictively forces to become a prostitute."

RECORDINGS
❖ Levine, Domingo, Scotto, Milnes, Alldis Chorus, National Philharmonic Orchestra (RCA) ❖ Chailly, Pavarotti, Caballé, Nucci, Kuhlmann, Welsh National Opera Chorus, National Philharmonic Orchestra (Decca) ❖

Un Ballo in Maschera

Giuseppe Verdi (1859)

They couldn't disguise their love!

In short: A man is discovered indulging in a moonlight tryst with his own wife, much to everyone else's amusement. As a result, he shoots his best friend.

Music
Ballo has all the emotional extremes of its predecessors *Rig*, *Trav* and *Trov* without the depth. But it is a vivid and varied score, including a rollicking Offenbachian finale to the first scene, a quasi-Wagnerian love duet, and a winsome pageboy straight out of *Die Fledermaus*. The thing goes at breakneck speed, and if it's hard to feel much sympathy for any of the characters one can at least admire the gusto with which they embrace their chosen methods of self-destruction.

Words
Amazingly, based on fact: to wit the 1792 assassination of Gustavus III of Sweden by his chief of staff Count Ankarström (though *he* took 13 days to die of gangrene). But the censors were jumpy and the setting had to be changed, not to mention the cast: the plotters, counts Horn and Ribbing, become a couple of unlikely negroes, Samuel and Tom, one of whose fathers has, unusually, had his castle confiscated by Riccardo. The librettist, Antonio Somma, astutely remained anonymous.

Important note
Owing to the (frankly rudimentary) disguises adopted by the characters at virtually every point in this opera, nobody ever recognises anyone else, despite the fact that they have known and in some cases been married to each other for many years.

Plot

Act I Riccardo, Governor of Boston, visits a fortune-teller named Ulrica to decide whether she should be deported as an illegal immigrant. Among those also present is his best friend Renato's wife Amelia, with whom Riccardo is in love. She, coincidentally, is asking Ulrica to cure her of her love for Riccardo, and is told to eat some weeds growing by the town gallows. When Riccardo's turn comes, Ulrica tells him he will be killed by the first person whose hand he shakes. Like an idiot he chooses Renato.

Act II Amelia hangs around the gallows at night collecting her weeds. While she is there Riccardo pops up and they bemoan their impossible love. Inconveniently, Renato now arrives to tell Riccardo that some conspirators are in the vicinity. Riccardo hurriedly covers Amelia up with her veil and asks Renato to escort her back to town while he legs it. On the way they run into the conspirators and Amelia's identity is revealed, a bit of a surprise for Renato but quite a lark for the baddies.

Act III Renato decides to kill both Amelia and Riccardo at the evening's masked ball, but succeeds only in the latter.

Don't ask

How come everyone knows they can find Riccardo at the gallows? Isn't it supposed to be a secret?

What the papers said

"A profanation in verse."

Crush Bar gambit

"Once you realise that Riccardo is thoroughly homosexual (like Gustavus himself) everything falls into place. His obviously chaste pursuit of Amelia is merely a cover for his rather more passionate relationship with his catamite, the page Oscar. The assassination is masterminded by homophobic elements in the court who trick the poor dupe Renato into carrying out the deed."

Recordings

❖ Abbado, Ricciarelli, Domingo, Bruson, Gruberova, La Scala (DG)
❖ Votto, Callas, di Stefano, Gobbi, Ratti, La Scala (EMI) ❖

The Barber of Seville

GIOACHINO ROSSINI (1816)

A prisoner in her home – but her heart was free!

In short: Count Almaviva gets his girl in spite of the local hairdresser's hamfisted attempts to help.

MUSIC

Rossini is the P.G. Wodehouse of opera: the most frightful scrapes always sort themselves out, and his high spirits leave you feeling much better after than you did before. The first act – a greatest hits medley – is finished off with one of opera's most exhilarating finales, a stageful of people (including a police squad) all doing their own thing increasingly frantically and loudly: it is a great relief when they all finish at roughly the same time. The jaunty insouciance of the music conceals a deal of subtlety, and is not above making fun of operatic conventions, as when the conspirators' means of escape is removed even as they rehearse one of those interminable "let's go" routines.

WORDS

A slapstick adaptation by Cesare Sterbini of the first and most farcical play of Beaumarchais's *Figaro* trilogy.

PLOT

Act I Count Almaviva has taken a fancy to Rosina, the ward of priapic old goat Dr Bartolo, who plans to marry her. After dressing up as an indigent student and singing well-received serenades beneath her balcony, Almaviva enlists the help of Figaro, the town barber and Bartolo's household handyman, to infiltrate him into the house. On Figaro's suggestion he presents himself at the house disguised as a drunken soldier with a billeting order. This is less than successful: a row ensues, the police turn up, and Almaviva narrowly escapes a night in the can.

Act II *Plan B: Almaviva comes back, this time purporting to be a singing teacher, standing in for Rosina's regular teacher Basilio who he claims is ill. He arranges a midnight elopement with Rosina. Figaro arrives to give Bartolo a shave and steals the key to the balcony. Inevitably, Basilio himself now appears – in perfect health – complicating matters. Bartolo, dimly realising something is up, sets off to fetch the registrar to marry him to Rosina. Almaviva and Figaro slip into the house through the balcony, Almaviva reveals his true identity to Rosina, the registrar appears and marries them. Bartolo, who has been detained removing a ladder from beneath the balcony, arrives late and accepts the situation with surprisingly good grace.*

DON'T ASK

Why exactly Count Almaviva thinks pretending to be an impecunious student is a smart idea.

FIRST NIGHT BLUES

Manifold: Almaviva's guitar was mistuned, Bartolo tripped over on his entrance and sang his first aria with his nose streaming blood, a cat somehow got in among the finale and caused mayhem (egged on by the crowd) and supporters of Paisiello's 1782 version of the opera hissed the show off the stage.

NOT MANY PEOPLE KNOW THAT

Oddly, considering the subject matter, Rossini neglected to shave while composing the piece (but then it only took him a fortnight).

CRUSH BAR GAMBIT

"*The Barber of Seville* is a proto-Marxist exposition of the capitalist crisis which heralds the revolutionary events of *The Marriage of Figaro*. Money has become the only signifier of human relations, and the consequent social breakdown is the artistic redaction of that predicted in the *Communist Manifesto*."

RECORDINGS
❖ Galliera, Callas, Gobbi, Alva, Philharmonia Chorus and Orchestra (EMI) ❖ Varviso, Berganza, Ansensi, Benelli, Naples Scarlatti Chorus and Orchestra (Decca) ❖

The Bartered Bride

BEDŘICH SMETANA (1866)

Czechs mate!

In short: *A highly dubious contract results in the writing-off of a debt and a marriage.*

MUSIC

The Czech national opera – even though Smetana was not a native Czech speaker. From the irresistible overture with its rushing string fugues, via catchy dances to duets and ensembles based on folksy rhythms, it is the most good-natured of operas, and sophisticated enough to appeal even to those immune to the charms of central European peasant culture. Using typical folk-song figures – major/minor shifts, repeated phrases, droning pedals and so on – rather than actual quotations, Smetana embellishes the music with twiddly woodwind groups, flowing string lines, a nice admixture of patter songs and even a spot of coloratura. Highlights: the jolly opening heel-down chorus, Jeník and Mařenka's duet and her melancholy lament before their courtly *Jako matka*; Act II has a relaxedly romantic duet between Vašek and Mařenka before Jeník and Kecal's jaunty double-act, and in Act III a good scene of mock drama is rounded off with Mařenka's swooning *Ten lásky sen* and subsequent quarrel with Jeník, a jovial polka.

WORDS

By Karel Sabina, a struggling nationalist poet.

PLOT

Act I Mařenka is in love with Jeník but is required to marry Vašek, a local idiot, apparently because her father is in debt to his, Mícha. A marriage broker, Kecal, has been employed to sort out the details.

Act II *Mařenka (incognito) runs into Vašek and convinces him that the last thing he wants is to marry that bitch Mařenka. Meanwhile Jeník promises Kecal (for a consideration) not to marry Mařenka, but only on condition that she marries Mícha's son.*

Act III *As it happens, there is a travelling circus in town, and by means of sexual blackmail Vašek is persuaded to fill in for the dancing bear, who is apparently in an advanced state of refreshment. Mařenka finds out about Jeník's agreement, is pretty hacked off, and agrees to marry Vašek. At this point Jeník reveals that he is in fact Mícha's son, albeit from a previous marriage, so according to the contract Mařenka can now marry him. Amazingly, everyone seems to accept this somewhat unsatisfactory state of affairs, and Kecal is laughed out of town.*

Don't ask
Are those promises of sexual favours received by Vašek ever honoured?

Revision notes
It started life as a two-act operetta with spoken dialogue (and was a flop on its first appearance); most of the best-known bits were added subsequently, and some removed, notably an Act III duet between the circus performers which Smetana took out before Emperor Franz Josef's visit, thinking it was too risqué. He needn't have bothered: old Franz walked out after Act I.

Crush Bar gambit
"It is full of the horrific undercurrents of peasant life: the tormenting of the village idiot, the blatantly anti-Semitic scapegoating of Kecal, the murky history of family abuse that has caused Jeník to run away in the first place, the hints of serial incest. This atmosphere of alienation is emphasised by the odd fact that nobody in this village seems to have been introduced to anybody else."

Recording
❖ Košler, Beňačková, Dvorský, Novák, Czech Philharmonic Chorus and Orchestra (Supraphon) ❖

Billy Budd

BENJAMIN BRITTEN (1951)

Rum, sodomy and the lash!

In short: *Everybody's favourite sailor is strung up following confusion between the name of a ship and the title of a revolutionary pamphlet.*

MUSIC

Typical Britten: big effects produced with extreme economy. Despite a large orchestra, instruments are used solo and in unusual combinations, so as not to drown the all-male cast, and for their individual qualities. The sea heaves gently in the background and the sailors sing wistful shanties with the flavour of negro spirituals. The atmosphere is tense, ambiguous, claustrophobic, relieved only by a burst of action in Act III (and by the captain's muster in Act I, subsequently cut by Britten after Ernest Newman had rudely compared it with *HMS Pinafore*). Less lyrical than *Peter Grimes*, it nonetheless has some wonderful tunes: the flogged novice's soprano sax, Billy's heartbreaking lullaby and soliloquy as he awaits execution, and the extraordinary sequence of chords as Vere reads him his sentence.

WORDS

By Eric Crozier and E.M. Forster, from Herman Melville's last novel. Forster, who had not published a novel since 1924 because of "weariness of the only subject that I both can and may treat – the love of men for women and *vice versa*" had in mind the redemptive nature of "good" homosexuality (ie, Billy's) over "bad" (Claggart's), but Britten toned this down, making the thing rather more interesting.

PLOT

Act I *1797. Billy, a keen and comely chap, is press-ganged onto HMS* Indomitable *from a merchantman,* The Rights o' Man. *The master-at-arms, Claggart – a pig – takes a dislike to him and details the ship's corporal, Squeak, to wind him up.*

Act II *Billy catches Squeak rifling his stuff and beats him up. There are witnesses, so Claggart has to have Squeak arrested. Plan B: he gets another sailor to try to incite Billy to mutiny. Billy sees him off as well.*

Act III *A French ship is sighted and* Indomitable *gives chase, but gets stuck in fog. Claggart tells Captain Vere that Billy is planning a mutiny. Vere hauls them both in. Billy has an inconvenient stammering attack, and answers the charges by nailing Claggart with a straight right to the temple, killing him stone dead. He is court-martialled and sentenced to swing.*

Act IV *Billy is strung up from the yardarm after forgiving the Captain. In the epilogue an aged Vere looks back and wonders where it all went wrong.*

ALSO KNOWN AS
Twilight of the Sods (Thomas Beecham);
The Bugger's Opera (William Walton).

COLIN WILSON'S VIEW
"There is no reason why innocence should not be a valid theme for music, but to dwell on it for 30 years argues a certain arrested development."

CRUSH BAR GAMBIT
"The paradox of Captain Vere is that he is simultaneously fighting the French and trapped within a wholly Voltairean *Weltanschauung* whose rationalism negates the very freedom of action it purports to promote. The meretricious enlightenment propagated by the French turns men into the dupes of an ineluctable fate: the opera's Christian message is that the route to true wisdom lies in the gift of free will."

RECORDINGS
❖ Britten, Glossop, Pears, Langdon, Shirley-Quirk, London Symphony Orchestra (London) ❖ Nagano, Hampson, Rolfe Johnson, Halvarson, Smythe, Hallé Chorus and Orchestra (Erato) ❖

La Bohème

GIACOMO PUCCINI (1896)

Their tiny assets were frozen!

In short: *Failure to pay the heating bill has serious consequences for a group of Parisians.*

MUSIC
Puccini's fourth opera, his most lyrical and best-loved. It lacks the hysteria of other works, its understatement encapsulated in Mimì's pianissimo death. *Bohème* has it all: sentimentality cut with comedy (viz the Act III love duet interrupted by Marcello and Musetta hurling insults at each other), wonderful painting of street life and icy Parisian dawns, expansive tunes (particularly *Che gelida manina* and *Mi chiamano Mimì*), an understated use of leitmotiv, and huge charm. Audiences were taken aback by this picture of contemporary lowlife, but these characters now seem among the most endearing in opera.

WORDS
Puccini's long-suffering collaborators Giacosa and Illica put together four scenes from Henry Murger's autobiographical notes on his dealings with various Parisian *cocottes* in the 1840s. (Murger took *la vie bohème* pretty seriously, once receiving a visitor in bed after lending his only trousers to a pal for an interview.)

PLOT
Act I *A group of unemployed flatmates decides to celebrate Christmas Eve in a rive gauche caff. One of them, Rodolfo, is slightly delayed and meets Mimì, a girl with poor circulation and a nasty cough. Having fallen in love, they set off to join the others.*

Act II *At the caff, everyone's high spirits are lowered by the arrival of Musetta, former girlfriend of one of their number (Marcello), with her latest sugar daddy, Alcindoro. It seems she is intent on effecting a reunion with Marcello, however: she sends Alcindoro off on an errand, whereupon the rest of them do a runner, leaving him to pick up their bill.*

Act III *A couple of months later, Mimi and Rodolfo are on the rocks (and Mimi still has that cough: she should see a doctor). They decide to stick it out till spring. Marcello, who now has a job, splits up with Musetta.*

Act IV *Rodolfo is back in his garret with Marcello (who no longer has a job). They are moping about their exes (both of whom are now set up with more financially viable prospects) when – hey presto – they both appear, though Mimi is pretty rough by this stage, so much so in fact that she pegs out before too long.*

DON'T ASK
Wouldn't Mimi be better off dying in relative comfort *chez* her new beau?

NOT MANY PEOPLE KNOW THAT
Puccini had been planning to write something based on a story by the Sicilian writer Verga, but lost enthusiasm when he was arrested as a spy by the British authorities in Malta while doing some research.

WHAT THE PAPERS SAID
"Not stimulating enough to be heard often."

NOT TO BE CONFUSED WITH
Leoncavallo's *Bohème*. Hearing that Leoncavallo was using Murger's book was all the impetus Puccini needed to do the same.

CRUSH BAR GAMBIT
"Obviously, it is a politico-economic satire on the naïve proto-syndicalism of these so-called Bohemians. Their dismal attempts at work in unproductive branches of the manufacturing sector are merely an extension of their juvenile attitude to rent and bills. Only Musetta understands that wealth-creation lies in service industries and in moving her assets from lower to higher-valued uses."

RECORDINGS
❖ Beecham, de los Angeles, Björling, Amara, Merrill, RCA Victor Chorus and Orchestra (EMI) ❖ Nagano, Te Kanawa, Leech, Titus, London Symphony Orchestra and Chorus (Erato) ❖

Boris Godunov

MODEST MUSORGSKY (1874)

Tsars in their eyes!

In short: *The Russians get sick of one psychopathic ruler, and enthusiastically welcome another.*

MUSIC

Completely different from Italian or German opera, the harmonically and rhythmically unclassifiable music of *Boris* comes partly from modal Russian church and folk idioms but mostly from the head of the self-taught composer. *Boris* uses a leitmotiv system of sorts, the accompaniments varied to alter the atmosphere; most of the singing is tuneful declamation, leavened with boisterous folk interludes, elemental choral scenes, and, in Act III, pseudo-European elegance. Almost anti-theatrical in its concentration on onstage reaction to offstage events, *Boris* is utterly compelling, its characters pithily alive, the hero a touching mixture of paternal kindness and doomed sinner.

WORDS

Nine scenes from Pushkin's Shakespearean play, supplemented by Karamzin's Russian history and – in the person of Rangoni – Musorgsky's imagination.

PLOT

Prelude *A rentamob tries to persuade Boris to accept the crown. After a proper show of reluctance, he does.*

Act I *Six years later, Pimen, a monk, tells his cellmate Grigory how Boris came to power by ordering the murder of Ivan the Terrible's seven-year-old son Dimitri twelve years back. Grigory (19) does some quick sums and begins to get ideas. A bit later, we come across Grigory and some drunken mendicants in a pub on the Lithuanian border. The cops are on his tail, but he gives them the slip.*

Act II *Boris is getting nasty nightmares about Dimitri, not helped when his unreliable aide Shuisky turns up to tell him that someone claiming to be Dimitri (ie, Grigory) is raising an army in Poland.*

Act III *In Poland, Grigory makes overtures to scary Marina Mniszech, and they are both worked over by creepy Jesuit Rangoni, who sees possibilities for Catholic advancement in Russia following Grigory's takeover.*

Act IV *Boris is insulted by a holy fool outside the Kremlin. Later he shows up out of his mind at a cabinet meeting. Pimen appears and tells Boris how Dimitri's grave has started working miracles. Boris dies. Grigory invades Russia, claiming to be Dimitri. He seems very popular, except with the holy fool who has somehow made the 400-mile trip from Moscow and sees bad things ahead.*

Sounds familiar
The official enquiry into Dimitri's death concluded that he "accidentally stabbed himself in the throat while playing with a knife".

Not many people know that
Grigory married Marina and was immediately recognised as Dimitri by the latter's mother. Following his death (butchered, incinerated and blasted from a cannon) a second "False Dimitri" appeared, whom Marina lost no time in affirming to be her husband. Shuisky also got to be Tsar for a bit.

What Tchaikovsky thought
"I consign it from the bottom of my heart to the devil; it is the most insipid and base parody on music."

Crush Bar gambit
"Musorgsky's invention of the ogre Rangoni brilliantly exposes the neurotic flaw at the heart of Slavophile mythology, a schizoid fear of contamination by the non-Russian undermined by the quasi-sexual allure of anything foreign. The pathological, paranoid need to invent an external threat is borne of a castration-type inferiority complex."

Recordings
❖ Abbado, Kocherga, Larin, Leiferkus, Ramey, Lipovšek, Berlin Philharmonic (Sony) ❖ Rostropovich, Raimondi, Polozov, Plishka, Vishnevskaya, Washington National Symphony Orchestra (Erato) ❖

Capriccio

RICHARD STRAUSS (1942)

Six characters in search of an opera!

In short: *Some idle French aristos unwisely flaunt their wealth shortly before the Revolution.*

MUSIC

Strauss's last and mellowest opera, written in his late seventies, is typified by the sound of the string sextet which forms its prelude: vaguely nostalgic, rich, restrained. A conversation-piece where the words need to be heard, the scoring is necessarily less lavish than usual, the tone more even and the climaxes fewer and soberer; but this is an intricate tapestry of pastiche, quotation, tuneful arioso and mood-painting, its centrepiece a fugue and two boisterous octets. The final orchestral scene and soprano outpouring are among Strauss's most lovely. By the way, the reason Strauss can often sound like a high-class film score is that many of his musical disciples (Max Steiner, Erich Korngold, etc), constrained to emigrate from Germany, wound up in Hollywood.

WORDS

Based on a libretto written by Giambattista Casti for Salieri. Casti was Lorenzo da Ponte's great rival, and seems to have had much in common with him: a priest who was expelled from Paris for writing pornographic poems, he spent time in St Petersburg as court poet to Catherine the Great and at Joseph II's Viennese court where he apparently procured virgins for Count Rosenberg, the director of court entertainments and Mozart's *bête noire*, before dying of colic in Paris "while cracking jokes". Stefan Zweig and Joseph Gregor both worked on the libretto before Strauss adapted it himself with the conductor Clemens Krauss.

PLOT

Act I *Somewhere near Paris, 1775; a dress rehearsal for the 27th birthday party of the widowed Countess Madeleine, to include entertainments provided* *by a composer, Flamand, and a playwright, Olivier, both of whom have the hots for her, plus a third from a director, La Roche. Olivier reads a sonnet to Madeleine and Flamand sets it to music, much to Olivier's disgust. She, however, likes it and arranges a rendezvous with Flamand the next morning.*

Act II *A dancer and some singers entertain everyone while they have a futile argument about the relative merits of music, words and drama in opera. To general ridicule La Roche outlines the plans for his party-piece. A proposal that Flamand, Olivier and La Roche write and stage an opera based on the day's events is accepted without enthusiasm. Madeleine thinks it might help her decide between Flamand and Olivier, but this seems unlikely.*

FIRST NIGHT BLUES
The première, in Munich, had to be played without an interval so the audience could get home before the nightly air-raid began at 10pm. The prelude was premièred at a bash given by Strauss's pal Baldur von Schirach, Hitler Youth pin-up and Gauleiter of Vienna (who got 20 years at Nuremberg).

STRANGE BUT TRUE
The opening was delayed from June to October to accommodate baritone Hans Hotter's hayfever.

WHAT THE CRITICS SAID
Often described as "a drawing-room comedy written in the shadow of Dachau".

CRUSH BAR GAMBIT
"These over-civilised epicures have reached such a level of aesthetic self-absorption that they no longer have the capacity for independent emotion, nor any handle on political reality. The 'entertainment' the servants are planning for Madeleine seems pretty certain to include a guillotine."

RECORDINGS
❖ Böhm, Janowitz, Fischer-Dieskau, Schreier, Prey, Bavarian Radio Symphony Orchestra (DG) ❖ Sawallisch, Schwarzkopf, Ludwig, Gedda, Fischer-Dieskau, Hotter, Ludwig, Philharmonia Orchestra (EMI) ❖

Carmen

GEORGES BIZET (1875)

No man could tame her – but they still tried!

In short: *A dim-witted corporal is comprehensively undone by an unreliable gypsy woman; he kills her.*

MUSIC

Verve and firecrackers from overture to final curtain: the tunes are so well-known it can be hard to see beyond them to the tragedy of poor old José. It is of course a byword for Spanishness (except among Spaniards) and Carmen's own music is the most wantonly sexy in the repertoire; but Bizet can also do an ensemble like no-one since Rossini, and juggles soloists, chorus and orchestra with the lightest of touches, handling the woodwind like a further set of voices. *Carmen* is a step along the path towards *verismo* and Puccini. Showstoppers (excluding the obvious ones): José and Micaela's Act I duet, *Parlez-moi de ma mère*; the tremendous Act II and Act III smugglers' ensembles.

WORDS

A vivid drama by Meilhac and Halévy, from the story by Prosper Mérimée, to be applauded as the most un-New Labour libretto ever: a paean to smoking, chronic sexual promiscuity, blood sports, racial stereotyping, non-payment of taxes and general social irresponsibility.

PLOT

Act I *José, a dragoon, is minding his own business outside the cigarette factory when Carmen (having a fag break with her workmates) chucks a flower at him. He is peculiarly bothered by this, but his sweetheart Micaela shows up and he resolves to marry her. Later he arrests Carmen for provoking a catfight in the factory. She persuades him to let her escape (incurring two months in the guardhouse for him) with unspecified promises of sexual favours.*

Act II *Released from chokey, José comes to redeem the said favours. Carmen, who is keeping a matador (Escamillo) and José's superior officer circling above* *her runway, so to speak, persuades José to desert the army and join her smuggler companions in the mountains. By now he is hopelessly smitten.*

Act III *In the mountains, José frets about what his old mother would think of it all. Furthermore, Carmen is getting tired of him – of which fact Escamillo helpfully pitches up to inform him. At this highly inconvenient moment José has to make a mercy dash to his dying mother's bedside, but he assures Carmen they will meet again.*

Act IV *José waylays Carmen outside the bullring where she's waiting for Escamillo to finish off the bull before seeing to her. Unable to handle this, José stabs her to death and collapses in despair upon her body.*

STRANGE BUT TRUE
The foolish French booed the first performance, except for *Toreador*, of which, while writing it, Bizet said: "They want manure – they can have it."

WHAT THE PAPERS SAID
"Another *Traviata*, with the redeeming features which may be discovered in that libretto carefully eliminated." (*Music Trade Review*)

CRUSH BAR GAMBIT
"Clearly, Carmen's capital crime is to subvert the gender paradigm; as a sexual consumer, she has usurped masculinity. She is of course doubly an outsider, being also a gypsy among Spaniards. Her death is, therefore, both necessary and desirable."

RECORDINGS
❖ Karajan, Baltsa, Carreras, van Dam, Ricciarelli, Paris Opera, Berlin Philharmonic (DG) ❖ Bernstein, Horne, McCracken, Krause, Maliponte, Metropolitan Opera (DG) ❖

Cav 'n' Pag

Cavalleria Rusticana PIETRO MASCAGNI (1890)
I Pagliacci RUGGERO LEONCAVALLO (1892)

They couldn't tell their arts from their elbows!

In short: *Two Italian women are unconscionably cavalier with their marriage vows, with fatal consequences.*

MUSIC

These irresistible *verismo* twins are the bloody entrails of Italian opera, two-and-a-half hours of basic instincts. *Cav* (Queen Victoria's favourite opera) is a crudely effective sit-trag, bargain-basement Bizet/Verdi that nonetheless includes all-time highlights in the Easter Hymn and Turiddu and Santuzza's duet. It is brilliantly paced: the spurts of action are larded with big chunks of scene-setting, and the tension is first cranked up and then relaxed by the intermezzo and Turiddu's jolly Neapolitan drinking song before the final mayhem. *Pag* is marginally more recherché, the result of Leoncavallo's analysis of *Cav*'s success, again deceptively calm before the storm with a nice line in slippery violins and a cute neo-classical take-off for the *commedia* music. Italian audiences regularly force poor Canio to encore *Vesti la giubba* three or four times, and the sanguinary climax is a shocker of stunning impact.

WORDS

Cav is from a story by Verga; Mascagni had a couple of mates run him up a libretto. *Pag* was sued for plagiarism of his play *La femme de Tabarin* by Catulle Mendès, whereupon Leoncavallo conveniently remembered that it was based on a case his magistrate father had once tried. Mendès, incidentally, was also accused of theft by one Paul Ferrier, who had written a play called *Tabarin*…

PLOT

Cav Santa, neither the bearded philanthropist nor the London socialite but a Sicilian peasant girl also known as Santuzza, has been impregnated and deserted by the drippy Turiddu, who helps his mum out in the local off-licence, *and whom Santa caught on the rebound when Turiddu's girl Lola hauled off and got married to travelling salesman Alfio while Turiddu was doing national service. Turiddu and Lola are now an (undercover) item again. Santa kindly informs Alfio of this, and he hurries off to kill Turiddu in time-honoured fashion. Santa moves into the wine trade with Turiddu's mum, since there is now, after all, a vacancy.*

Pag *A dysfunctional troupe of travelling players arrives in a Calabrian town. Nedda (Columbine), married to Canio (Clown), makes plans for an after-show runner with local boy Silvio. Canio gets wind that something is up and wigs out during the performance, killing Nedda, Silvio and the show stone dead.*

DON'T ASK
Where's this rustic cavalry, then?

STRANGE BUT TRUE
Puccini and the publisher Ricordi rejected *Cav* before it won first prize in a competition for one-acters; the same pair also sacked Leoncavallo from the team of writers employed on Puccini's *Manon Lescaut*.

NOT MANY PEOPLE KNOW THAT
The compliant Mascagni succeeded Toscanini as music director of La Scala – and became Mussolini's official composer – when the latter refused to play *Giovinezza*, the Fascist anthem, before performances.

WHAT THE CRITICS SAID (OF PAG)
"Abominably commonplace." (Vincent d'Indy)

CRUSH BAR GAMBIT
"This is crude right-wing propaganda about the pernicious influence of excessive leisure and its associated drunkenness on the peasantry. *Cav* takes place at Easter, *Pag* at the Assumption; the inference is that if everyone were soberly working in the fields none of this trouble would have happened."

RECORDINGS
❖ Serafin, Callas, di Stefano, Panerai, Gobbi, La Scala Chorus and Orchestra (EMI) ❖ Muti, Caballé, Scotto, Carreras, Manuguerra, Philharmonia Orchestra (EMI) ❖

La Cenerentola

Gioachino Rossini (1817)

Skivvy cleans up!

In short: *A prince keen on fancy-dress tomfoolery bankrupts a local baron and steals his scullery-maid.*

Music

Composed in a hurry (three weeks) when a previous commission was vetoed by the Roman censor, it was Rossini's nineteenth opera, his sixth within 15 months, and his last *buffa* – all at the age of 25. Largely composed of explosive ensembles, breathless patter songs and coloratura fireworks, it is not performed as much as it should be owing to the difficulty of finding an alto and high tenor who can handle it. From the concert-standard overture (lifted from his earlier opera *La Gazzetta*) to Cinders's flowery triumph it is as consistently a joy as *The Barber of Seville*, and the second-act ensemble *Questo è un nodo avviluppato*, a staccato, trilling canon shot through with flashes of fioritura, beats even that opera for cheek. Rossini's usual light-fingered scoring is much in evidence, the orchestra playing tag like a troupe of jugglers on speed.

Words

By Jacopo Ferretti, who "came up with" the idea at short notice on Christmas Eve 1816. One of the best and wittiest of comic librettos, given added piquancy by a helping of genuine needle between the characters.

Plot

Act I *Cinders, real name Angelina, kept as a drudge by her stepfather Baron Magnifico and his ghastly daughters, is hacked off when the others are invited to a thrash by the local prince, Ramiro, who needs to find a wife fastish or lose his inheritance. Ramiro comes to pick the girls up disguised as his valet and runs into Cinders, with immediate effect. She wangles a last-minute invite from Ramiro's tutor Alidoro, a fairy-godmother stand-in. At the party everyone thinks there's something vaguely familiar about her but can't quite put their*

38

finger on it. Meanwhile Ramiro's valet, Dandini (dressed as the prince, obviously) checks out the sisters.

Act II *Ramiro tells the incognito Cinders he fancies her, but she, playing hard to get, gives him one of her bracelets, tells him he'll have to hunt her down to complete the set, and leaves. Alidoro organises a carriage-crash for Ramiro (by now back in uniform) outside her front door, and nature takes its course – a headache for Don Magnifico, who has blown Cinders's inheritance and now needs to find a dowry.*

WHAT, NO PUMPKINS?
Ferretti claimed the lack of fairy godmothers, glass slippers, etc, was a concession to delicate Roman (ie, Papal) sensibilities. It would be more accurate to say it was because he'd copied the plot from Felice Romani's libretto for *Agatina*, by Pavesi, which Romani stole from Isouard's *Cendrillon*, which in turn owed quite a lot to Richardson's novel *Pamela, or Virtue Rewarded*.

NOT MANY PEOPLE KNOW THAT
It was the first opera staged in Australia (1844).

WHAT BYRON THOUGHT
"The picture would be better painted if the painter had taken more pains."

CRUSH BAR GAMBIT
"The opera's subtitle, *Goodness Triumphant*, is of course deeply sarcastic. Cinderella turns from a model of humility into a monster of social pretension, her growing artificiality emphasised by the way her music changes from unaffected simplicity to the outrageous, crowing coloratura of the last scene. This is a society with a pathological need to corrupt innocence."

RECORDINGS
❖ Abbado, Berganza, Alva, Capecchi, London Symphony Orchestra, Scottish Opera Chorus (DG) ❖ Chailly, Bartoli, Mateuzzi, Corbelli, Bologna Chorus and Orchestra (Decca) ❖

La Clemenza di Tito

Wolfgang Amadeus Mozart (1791)

Adored by all – and they all wanted him dead!

In short: Tito (not the Yugoslavian dictator but the obscure-yet-exceptionally-nice Roman emperor better known as Titus) is the object of a botched assassination attempt by his bride-to-be and his best friend.

Music

Mozart's last opera, composed partly on a coach journey from Vienna to Prague, where it was performed at the coronation of Leopold II. It is *opera seria*: more moral edification and an excuse for vocal show-offery than drama. Mozart is in repentance-and-forgiveness mode, as at the end of *Figaro* and in bits of *Magic Flute* and the *Requiem*, and the music has the same luminous simplicity. The extraordinary economy with which it is done has led some to think he wrote *Tito* in his sleep, but this is music which grows on you and absolutely transcends the terrible libretto (also, impossible to sleep on 18th-century coaches). Showstoppers: Annius and Servilia's sweet love duet. The Act I finale: soloists and chorus together contemplate the fire engulfing the Capitol. Sextus's and Vitellia's arias accompanied by fancy clarinet/ basset-horn *obbligati* written for Mozart's old pal Anton Stadler.

Words

A toadying text by the universal 18th-century librettist Metastasio, much beloved of German princelings: it had already been set 40 times before Mozart got his hands on it.

Plot

Act I (a) Vitellia, who loves Titus, incites Titus's best friend Sextus, who loves Vitellia (but is played by a woman), to burn down the Capitol (with Titus in it) since Titus has spurned Vitellia and is apparently about to marry one Berenice;

(b) Sextus's friend Annius (also played by a woman), who loves Servilia (Sextus's sister), reveals that Titus has given Berenice the heave-ho, so Vitellia countermands her orders to Sextus, thinking she's next in line; however,

(c) Titus now decides to marry Servilia, but she tells him her heart belongs to Annius. Titus is very understanding. Vitellia, a bit behind with the news, again gives Sextus the go-ahead for the assassination. He sets off, reluctantly;

(d) Vitellia discovers that Titus plans to marry her after all (indeed, today). But it is too late, Sextus has started a rebellion, the Capitol is in flames and there are reports that Titus is dead.

Act II *The reports are exaggerated: Titus is OK. Sextus is arrested and condemned to become the* pasto infelice *of the lions. At the Colosseum the frightfully noble Titus is about to set him free when Vitellia rushes into the royal box and tells Titus she was the real author of the plot. Titus, taking a deep breath, forgives everybody anyway.*

DON'T ASK
Who the hell does Titus thinks he's impressing with all this magnanimity?

STRANGE BUT TRUE
Salieri was first choice for the commission, but turned it down – five times. Leo's (Italian) wife called it "a German pig's breakfast".

CRUSH BAR GAMBIT
"Amazingly, most people think *Tito* is grotesquely sycophantic; in fact, *mutatis mutandis*, it is as profoundly revolutionary as *Figaro*. Leo's sister Antoinette had been arrested in France a couple of months before his coronation. There is an implicit warning: from now on, rulers have to be as perfectly super as Titus, and even then, they may not be safe."

RECORDINGS
❖ Davis, Baker, Minton, Burrows, von Stade, Covent Garden (Philips) ❖ Muti, Vaness, Ziegler, Winbergh, Barbaux, Vienna State Opera (EMI: live at Salzburg) ❖

The Coronation of Poppea

CLAUDIO MONTEVERDI (1642)

There's no place like Rome!

In short: An ambitious woman with no eye for a pattern marries a man with a marked tendency to kill his nearest and dearest.

MUSIC

Opera in its infancy, and music is the handmaid of words: *Poppea* is a play set to music. The music is mostly monodic, a single vocal line over a more or less simple continuo bass, varying between free arioso and more measured arias, their verses often divided by orchestral ritornellos. Within this apparently narrow musical range there is an astonishing variety of expression: Poppea is wantonly sexy, Octavia distraught, Otto wistful, Nero capricious, Seneca a miserable old git. There is a very Venetian juxtaposition of pathos and farce, such as Seneca's death (preceded by a comic madrigal by his pupils) followed by a sweet (and very naughty) love scene between a page and his girl, and Nero and Lucan's raucous drinking session.

WORDS

An astonishingly amoral text by Giovanni Busenello, drawn from Tacitus, with some of the most unpleasant characters in opera outside *The Ring*. It is presented as a trial of strength between the goddesses of Love, Fortune and Virtue (no prizes for guessing who wins).

PLOT

Act I Otto returns home to find his wife Poppea in bed with another man. Unluckily for him, it is Nero. Otto's old flame Drusilla catches him on the rebound. Seneca tells Nero's wife Octavia she better find herself a boyfriend.

Act II Irritated by Seneca's behaviour, Nero sends a message asking him to kill himself. Seneca, being a Stoic, does; Nero celebrates by getting pissed with the poet

Lucan. Octavia tells Otto she would appreciate it if he killed Poppea. He obligingly sets off to do so, having borrowed Drusilla's clothes, for some reason, but fails.

Act III *Drusilla is arrested in a classic case of mistaken identity. Otto then gives himself up, grasses on Octavia, and he and Drusilla argue about which of them should be executed. Nero exiles them both and has Octavia killed instead. Poppea marries Nero and is crowned empress.*

WHAT HAPPENED NEXT

Poppea got pregnant, but Nero stayed in character and kicked her to death.

DON'T ASK

Don't you think Seneca ought at least to check that message is genuine before topping himself?

STRANGE BUT TRUE

The opera's most celebrated music, Nero and Poppea's final duet *Pur ti miro*, is not by Monteverdi (nor the words by Busenello), rather (probably) by one Benedetto Ferrari.

GENDER CONFUSION

Total. Nero, often a mezzo-soprano though occasionally a tenor (and sometimes a counter-tenor), was originally a castrato, rather like Otto, who is sometimes a baritone (which must cause trouble when he borrows Drusilla's clothes). Poppea's nurse, Arnalta, was a tenor to begin with but is now often an alto (of either sex). Seneca is a bass, but nobody seems to be interested in him.

CRUSH BAR GAMBIT

"*Poppea* is the pathogenic moment that establishes the Right to Love as the lodestone of opera. The struggle between id and superego, personified as Amore and Virtù, is over before it has begun: from now on, the hysterical egoists of opera can pursue their desires unrestrained by any sense of morality or regard for the norms of civilised behaviour."

RECORDINGS

❖ Harnoncourt, Donath, Söderström, Berberian, Lucciardi, Concentus Musicus Wien (Teldec) ❖ Gardiner, McNair, von Otter, Hanchard, Chance, English Baroque Soloists (Archiv) ❖

Così fan tutte

WOLFGANG AMADEUS MOZART (1790)

They played away – on a sticky wicket!

In short: *Two singularly unobservant sisters fail to notice that the glamorous strangers they are about to marry are their boyfriends in disguise, and that their maid is a serial transvestite.*

MUSIC

On the face of it, *Così* is the lightest of the Mozart/da Ponte comedies, but this is an opera where nothing is quite what it seems. A frisky overture, all chirruping oboes and bassoons, sets the scene; sentimental music is undercut by laughing woodwind, and moments of pure *buffa* suddenly cloud over. Maybe there are fewer examples of heavenly inspiration than in *Figaro* or *Don Giovanni*, and there is more sitcom and slapstick than the character comedy of those operas, but in *Soave sia il vento* Mozart wrote his most ecstatic trio, undulating strings imitating the gentle swell of the sea and the two sopranos soaring above like guiding spirits. As befits a six-hander, the magic lies in the ensembles, where the characters' murky motives can be best expressed.

WORDS

An expanded anecdote worked into a libretto of humane if un-pc cynicism by Lorenzo da Ponte, the ex-Jewish-unfrocked-abbé philanderer. One in-joke is that Dorabella and Fiordiligi, the sisters from Ferrara, were sung at the première by two (supposed) sisters from Ferrara, one of whom was da Ponte's mistress, Adriana Ferrarese. Mozart was underwhelmed by her talents but still gave her one of the most reef-strewn soprano arias ever written, *Come scoglio*, a hideously difficult *opera seria* pastiche.

PLOT

Act I *Starry-eyed soldiers Guglielmo and Ferrando make a bet with Alfonso (a curmudgeon) that their girlfriends are incapable of being unfaithful. Alfonso arranges for the lads to be apparently sent off to war, then has them dress up* *as a pair of Albanians and make overtures to each other's girl. The overtures are unsuccessful.*

Act II *Under prompting from their* soubrette *of a maid, Despina, the sisters decide they may as well have some fun while the chaps are away. Within about five minutes things have rather got out of hand and they have fallen in love and agreed to marry the Albanians. Whereupon the boyfriends, to considerable embarrassment, arrive home from the war (which would appear to have lasted less than a day), accept the girls' apologies, and marry them anyway, presumably in the original configurations, though this is not entirely clear.*

STRANGE BUT TRUE

The 19th century was so outraged by the slurs on the morals of womankind that a German translation had Despina letting the girls in on the deception (despite the fact that she doesn't recognise the boyfriends any more than her mistresses).

WHAT THE PAPERS SAID

"Trivial and scandalous, degrading to the romantic idealization of women."

CRUSH BAR GAMBIT

"*Così* manages to be both subversive and proto-fascist: while specifically suggesting that monogamy is artificial and unsustainable, it simultaneously decries the corrupting influence of servants and intellectuals on social morality. Written in the shadow of French revolutionary terror, *Così* formulates the thesis of a dialectic that will find its synthesis in Auschwitz."

RECORDINGS

❖ Gardiner, Roocroft, Mannion, Trost, Gilfry, Monteverdi Chorus, English Baroque Soloists (Archiv) ❖ Böhm, Schwarzkopf, Ludwig, Kraus, Taddei, Philharmonia Chorus and Orchestra (EMI) ❖

The Cunning Little Vixen

Leoš Janáček (1924)

Dances with voles!

In short: *An oversexed Moravian neighbourhood witnesses a fox's conversion into a fur stole.*

MUSIC

Janáček's translucent harmonies and scoring bring the forest to life in this sunny, vivid bucolic romp. (This is a man who on a visit to London zoo transcribed the songs of monkeys, seals and walruses.) Now lyrical, now chatty, the scenes from the vixen's short life are held together by the composer's characteristic short motifs. There is a wistfulness to much of the music (he was nearly 70 when he wrote the opera) and a lavish use of modes and lilting, folkish rhythms. The orchestral interludes are particularly magical: playful woodwind depicting the birds and dancing insects in the summer forest in a slippery *ländler*, string writing of almost Viennese romanticism, and a final scene of pantheistic ecstasy (played at the composer's funeral).

WORDS

Janáček's daily introduced him to a strip-cartoon in the local paper with unusually carefree words by the future wife-murderer and suicide Rudolf Těsnohlídek, and he was so smitten with the story he decided to turn it into an opera. The Czech title is *The Adventures of Vixen Sharpears*, and it is written in Moravian dialect: as a result, Prague has always been rather sniffy about it. Part *Wind in the Willows*, part *Midsummer Night's Dream*, the animals are identified with various local humans, for example the badger and priest are sung by the same character.

PLOT

Act I A dipsomaniac gamekeeper having a snooze in the forest snaffles a fox-cub and takes her home as a pet. After fending off the sexual advances of the gamekeeper's dachshund and attacking his children Sharpears (for it is she) incites the chickens to revolution before massacring them, and sensibly does a quick runner back to the forest.

Act II Sharpears evicts a badger from his set by using it as a public convenience, and moves in. Following a prolonged drinking session with the gamekeeper, the local schoolmaster and priest indulge in amorous reveries in the forest, where Sharpears encourages the former in a sexual assault upon a sunflower he mistakes for his former girlfriend. A local fox makes advances which lead with sad inevitability from a rabbit-based supper to pregnancy and a shotgun wedding conducted by a woodpecker.

Act III Sharpears foolishly gets herself shot by the local poacher, who gives the resulting stole to his bride, the schoolmaster's ex (not the sunflower). The gamekeeper runs into her cubs in the forest, but is too drunk and decrepit by now to catch them.

DON'T ASK
Hunting, fur coats, drunks with shotguns … haven't these people ever heard of New Labour?

NOT MANY PEOPLE KNOW THAT
Sharpears was known as Bystronožka (Fleetfoot) until a copyist's typo improved her hearing.

UNIQUE SELLING POINT
One of the few operas in which one member of the cast (Frog) is required to jump on the nose of another (Gamekeeper). Perhaps as a result, most stagings have been disastrous.

CRUSH BAR GAMBIT
"Hardly a cuddly little bundle, Sharpears is in fact a crypto-Trotskyist agitator and the opera a hidden satire on recent events in Russia. Her Marxist-Leninist indoctrination of the hens is followed in classic style by their massacre; the badger/priest is first exiled and then, presumably, shot."

RECORDING
❖ Mackerras, Popp, Randová, Jedlička, Vienna Philharmonic (Decca) ❖

Dialogues des Carmélites

FRANCIS POULENC (1956)

Martyred – for hearing the Mass!

In short: *A neurasthenic nun overcomes her timidity to join her sisters on the scaffold.*

MUSIC

Counter-revolutionary, against both Robespierre and Schönberg: tonal, tuneful, dignified. The style is restrained sensuousness, dynamically and rhythmically measured except at moments of great stress. The nuns' music has an 18th-century limpidity, the orchestra dominated by wind instruments. In this most spiritual of operas the music is a gloss on the words and never obscures them – a lesson Poulenc learned from Monteverdi; bits of the score sound like a sane version of Musorgsky. Poulenc makes his unfashionable points with a conviction that carries along all but the most curmudgeonly of listeners. Showstoppers: the Latin hymns that punctuate the action, in particular the harrowing final ascent of the scaffold; the Prioress's startling death scene; the new Prioress's calming sermon to the nuns in prison, a good example of grace under pressure.

WORDS

An intended film script by Georges Bernanos, based on the true story of the Carmelite nuns of Compiègne, near Paris. A meditation on the point of religion and prayer, the workings of grace and the overcoming of fear and self-hatred, conducted, as the title implies, via the nuns' conversations.

PLOT

Act I *The French Revolution is just getting into its swing. Timorous Blanche decides to join a convent to escape the shocks of the world (NB dramatic irony) after a hairy experience with a revolutionary mob. The Prioress has her doubts* about Blanche's motivation, entrusts her to the care of strict-but-kind Mother Marie, then dies a painful and shocking death.

Act II Sister Constance (the Julie Andrews of the outfit) tells Blanche of a dream she has had that they will die on the same day; Blanche takes this badly. Blanche's brother tries to persuade her to leave the convent for her safety; she refuses, pretending to be brave. The convent is besieged by baying hordes and the nuns are ordered out.

Act III The convent has been sacked and the Prioress arrested. The nuns get ready for martyrdom; Blanche, terrified, runs home to Papa, but he has been executed and she takes refuge as a servant. Mother Marie tracks her down and urges her to rejoin her sisters. Blanche is not keen. The sisters are condemned to death (crime: liberticide). They process to the guillotine singing the Salve Regina. One by one their voices are snuffed out, then at last Blanche appears, elbows her way through the crowd and joins Constance on the scaffold.

Crush Bar gambit
"*Au fond, Carmelites* is about the impossibility of true communication among a nation as profligate with words as the French. Faced with something that transcends their revolutionary waffle the mob descends to a pre-linguistic chaos. In the end their only response is the meaningless, repetitive noise of the guillotine. Poulenc is condemning the French eagerness to subordinate sense to intellect and to forget about humanity."

RECORDINGS
❖ Dervaux, Duval, Crespin, Berton, Paris Opera (EMI: original cast)
❖ Nagano, Dubosc, Fournier, Gorr, Lyons Opera (EMI/Virgin) ❖

Dido and Aeneas

HENRY PURCELL (1684?)

Catharsis in Carthage!

In short: *A Trojan refugee spends the night with a North African queen and then deserts her citing a prior engagement in Italy. She dies.*

MUSIC

From the aching suspensions of the overture to Dido's last lament this is a little masterpiece of sadness, its small scale and chamber orchestra making it feel like an intrusion on private grief. It has been described as *Tristan and Isolde* in an hour, not only because of the final *Liebestod*, but also because Purcell paid more attention to word-painting than anybody until Wagner. It's not all gloom, however: Dido's sister has some perky tunes, the witches are gleefully malevolent, the chorus does a lot of work and even the rather ghastly Aeneas has his moments. Purcell was fond of composing his tunes over a repeating ground bass, and the results are harmonically daring and highly expressive. *Dido* was long thought to have been composed for a Chelsea girls' school in 1689; now scholarly opinion seems to be that it was written somewhat earlier for Charles II's court. Showstoppers: the witches' first scene; the jolly jack tars' song and hornpipe; Dido's lament, with its plangent appoggiaturas, and the subsequent heartbroken chorus and playout.

WORDS

Future poet laureate Nahum Tate's script has attracted a lot of flak, mostly because its idiocies are in English rather than Italian. But it does the job concisely and contains some rather neat turns of phrase; and he did add the witches to Vergil's story, a nice touch.

PLOT

Act I Aeneas has pitched up in Carthage following a hurried exit from Troy. Dido, the local queen, is urged by her sister Belinda to marry him. She has justifiable doubts about him, but Aeneas wins her over, the charmer.

Act II *A bunch of witches with a grudge against Dido arrange a surprise visit from Mercury – or god-o-gram – to tell Aeneas to get on with it and found Rome. Dido and Aeneas organise a picnic in the countryside, but it rains.*

Act III *Aeneas tells Dido – somewhat unconvincingly – that the gods are insisting on his Italian trip. They quarrel, he changes his mind, but too late: she is having none of it. He goes. She dies, apparently of natural causes.*

DON'T ASK
Belinda – is that a regular Carthaginian name, then?

STRANGE BUT TRUE
The opera disappeared from view for ages, perhaps suppressed by Purcell himself when unflattering comparisons were drawn between Aeneas and Dido and King Billy and Queen Mary.

UNIQUE SELLING POINT
Probably the only opera in which rain stops play.

CRUSH BAR GAMBIT
"*Dido* is of course religious philippic masquerading as drama. Aeneas represents the clerico-fascist James II, in league with his clique of Franco-Papist witches, and the havoc he wreaks on the court the inevitable result of a foreign-backed theocracy. No coincidence he slinks off to Rome at the end."

RECORDINGS
❖ Pinnock, von Otter, Varcoe, Dawson, Rogers, English Concert Choir and Orchestra (Archiv) ❖ Parrott, Kirkby, Thomas, Nelson, Noorman, Taverner Choir and Players (Chandos) ❖

Don Carlos

GIUSEPPE VERDI (1867, REVISED 1884)

Her heart belonged to daddy!

In short: *A Spanish Prince's excessive love for his stepmother leads to his best friend's death.*

MUSIC

Verdi's most ambitious opera – some would say his greatest – looks an unwieldy beast, a three-and-a-half-hour grand opera in the dreaded French tradition. But its heart lies in the immense drama of soliloquies, duets and ensembles pitting church against state, heart against head, tyranny against compassion. Generally performed in a composite Italian version of its various rewrites, it is full of marvellous characterisation and stunning scenes including the *auto-da-fé* and the most heartwarming male-bonding in opera between Carlos and Rodrigo. The overwhelmingly dark colours are relieved by some nice Act II Spanish frippery, including the Veil Song.

WORDS

From Schiller's 1787 play, itself based on a 17th-century anti-clerical tract surprisingly written by the Abbé César de St-Réal. Libretto by Joseph Méry and Camille du Locle, translated into Italian for later productions.

PLOT

Act I *Fontainebleau, 1559. While a peace summit takes place in the palace, Don Carlos, Infante of Spain, lurks in the woods and runs into Elisabeth de Valois, his intended. They hit it off like billyo. Sadly, the peace treaty unexpectedly stipulates that she must marry his father, the frightful Philip II, instead. Gloom all round.*

Act II *Back in Spain, Carlos mopes. He tells his troubles to his chum Rodrigo, who suggests they both go to Flanders to give a hand to the pro-independence guerrillas there. Elisabeth says she'll put in a word with Philip, who appoints Rodrigo his PA.*

Act III *In a distressing mix-up Carlos trysts with Princess Eboli – a flirt who fancies him rotten – under the impression that she is Elisabeth. When they've straightened things out she flies off the handle and plots revenge. Rodrigo, realising Carlos is heading for trouble, gets him to hand over all incriminating documentation re Flemish insurrections, etc. Later, during a public incineration of heretics, Carlos loses the plot and starts waving his sword at Philip. Rodrigo relieves him of it.*

Act IV *Philip OKs Carlos's execution with the Grand Inquisitor, then inquires of Elisabeth why on earth she is carrying around a photo of Carlos (of which Eboli has helpfully informed him). She protests her innocence, and fires Eboli. Rodrigo visits Carlos in prison to say goodbye: he's framed himself to get Carlos off the hook. Sure enough, he is shot during their chat by an Inquisition hit-man. Carlos is released.*

Act V *Elisabeth and Carlos have a final get-together in a monastery cloister, beside the tomb of Charles V (Carlos's grandpa). They are interrupted by Philip and the Grand Inquisitor, come to arrest them both. At this point, who should turn up but Charles V himself, dead these 20 years, who drags Carlos to safety in the monastery.*

Don't ask
Er, *now* what?

What Bizet thought
"Very bad … no melody."

Crush Bar gambit
"This rewrite of history makes Hollywood look like Holy Writ. Elisabeth was 14 at the time of her marriage to Philip, and seems most unlikely to have fallen in love with the psychopathic one-legged epileptic hunchback Carlos, who finally died from drinking too much cold water with his supper."

Recordings
❖ Giulini, Domingo, Caballé, Raimondi, Verrett, Milnes, Ambrosian Opera Chorus, Covent Garden (EMI) ❖ Levine, Furlanetto, Millo, Zajick, Sylvester, Chernov, Ramey, Battle, Metropolitan Chorus and Orchestra (Sony) ❖

Don Giovanni

WOLFGANG AMADEUS MOZART (1787)

Meet the host from hell!

In short: *Two men accept each other's dinner invitations, though neither is hungry, and both are late.*

MUSIC

The overture's thunderous D minor chords announce that this *dramma giocoso* isn't going to be sunshine all the way, and indeed the palpable terror of the Commendatore's appearance is something completely new in opera, as are the trombones that herald it. The mechanics of the plot – attempted rape, murder, oaths of vengeance – are got out of the way in short order and the comic capers of Giovanni's attempts to add to his 2,065 conquests take over. His main weapon is music itself, hence the difference between his one-dimensional solo efforts and the beguiling spells he weaves whenever a woman pops up over the horizon. The score is full of jokes, as when Giovanni and Leporello discuss their supper to the strains of recent operatic hits (including *Figaro*). Mozart's use of accompanied recit reaches new dramatic heights, the cast is neatly divided between serious and *buffo* characters, and few would argue with E.T.A. Hoffman's description of it as "the opera of operas". Showstoppers: there's no choosing between the arias. The episodic finale of Act I is a 20-minute masterpiece containing the opera's clever hinge, three orchestras playing dance tunes in different time signatures, leading to almost total musical disintegration.

WORDS

A semi-autobiographical number by Lorenzo da Ponte, the lecherous priest who was in Vienna on the run from a seven-year prison sentence for adultery and public concubinage in Venice. Curiously, he was instrumental in making *Don Giovanni* the first of Mozart's operas to be performed in North America when he quit his subsequent job as a distiller and set up an opera house in New York.

PLOT

Act I *Giovanni, a bounder, is constrained to kill Anna's father in self-defence following an (apparently) botched attempt upon the former's virtue. She and her weedy boyfriend Ottavio swear to avenge the silly old man. Giovanni has a difficult interview with an ex-girlfriend, Elvira, who then rudely interrupts him when he's getting on quite nicely with a flighty peasant girl. At a party that evening he is cornered by Anna and her friends, but with one bound he is free.*

Act II *Following a dalliance with Elvira's maid Giovanni finds himself in a churchyard with a statue of Anna's father, whom he politely invites to supper, although it is already 2am. There is surprise all round when the statue appears for the appointment and takes Giovanni off for a barbeque.*

STRANGE BUT TRUE

Mozart wrote the overture with a hangover between 5am and 7am on the day of the dress rehearsal.

NOT MANY PEOPLE KNOW THAT

The original play about the Don, *El burlador de Sevilla*, was written by a 17th-century Spanish monk, Tirso de Molina, to illustrate some nice theological points made at the Council of Trent.

CRUSH BAR GAMBIT

"Giovanni's downfall seems even more unfair when you consider the sterling work he does as psychotherapist-in-the-community, successfully treating the neurotic masochist Elvira, the frigid, father-fixated Anna, Ottavio the repressed homosexual, Zerlina the nymphomaniac hysteric and Masetto the alcoholic wife-beater."

RECORDINGS

❖ Giulini, Sutherland, Waechter, Alva, Schwarzkopf, Philharmonia Chorus and Orchestra (EMI) ❖ Davis, Wixell, Arroyo, Te Kanawa, Freni, Burrows, Covent Garden (Philips) ❖

Don Pasquale

GAETANO DONIZETTI (1843)

Marry at leisure – repent in haste!

In short: An impoverished serial wife snares her latest victims.

MUSIC

Donizetti lied that he composed this, his sixty-third opera, in eleven days:
actually it took more like three months. It might lack *L'Elisir d'Amore*'s soft
heart and characters you care about, but musically is the more finished
product and is packed with incidental pleasures: the accompanied recitative
with its sighing sixths, refugees from Mozart's *Requiem*, before the marriage,
the swaying, sentimental tune during it, the irrepressible orchestra that goes
its own sweet way behind the patter-songs. Top tunes: the Rossinian Act I
finale, full of vocal and instrumental nuances; the tremendous Act II finale;
Pasquale and Malatesta's duet *Cheti, cheti*, the ultimate patter-song; and
Norina and Ernesto's *Tornami a dir*, a sweet love duet in parallel sixths.

WORDS

More or less a straight steal from *Ser Marc'Antonio*, an 1810 opera by
Pavesi with libretto by Anelli, from Ben Jonson's play *Epicoene, or
the Silent Woman*. Giovanni Ruffini, a Mazzinian exile working in Paris
for a manufacturer of waterproofing soap, did the cut-and-paste job,
but Donizetti made his life such a misery that he refused to have his name
on the opera, for which credit was then claimed by one Michaele Accursi,
a fellow exile working as a double agent for both Mazzini and the Pope.

PLOT

Act I *Pasquale, a well-meaning buffoon, intends to dissuade his irritating
nephew Ernesto from marrying a gold-digging widow named Norina by getting
married himself and thereby disinheriting the boy. Pasquale's supposed friend
Dr Malatesta undertakes to provide a bride, allegedly his sister Sofronia, fresh
from a convent.*

Act II *Ernesto, who seems not to be in on the plot, bemoans his fate. Malatesta presents the wilting Sofronia to Pasquale; actually, of course, it is the dreaded Norina. They get married, whereupon Norina slips back into character and starts acting up.*

Act III *Having had her spend all his money (and been refused his conjugal rights) Pasquale attempts to ambush Sofronia and her fancy-man in the shrubbery. He fails. By now he is desperate to dump her, but the only way he can persuade her to leave is by allowing Ernesto to marry Norina, whom Sofronia cannot abide. Sofronia doffs her disguise. Pasquale laughs it off (hollowly, you might think) and a moral (beware the mid-to-late-life crisis) is somewhat unconvincingly drawn.*

DON'T ASK
Where *did* that chorus in the shrubbery spring from?

WHAT THE CRITICS SAID
"This Italian does not go without success. His talent is great but even greater is his fecundity, in which he is exceeded only by rabbits."
(Heinrich Heine in the *Augsburg Gazette*)

NOT TO BE CONFUSED WITH
Die schweigsame Frau, by Richard Strauss, also based on *Epicoene*.

CRUSH BAR GAMBIT
"The radical Donizetti is as usual making a point about the inherent contradictions of capitalism, namely the way that money's need to perpetuate itself and its innate tendency to stagnate can only be overcome by an illegal contract exacted under duress in breach of trust by Pasquale's doctor, seriously abusing his fiduciary position."

RECORDINGS
❖ R. Abbado, Bruson, Mei, Allen, Lopardo, Bavarian Radio Chorus, Munich Radio Orchestra (RCA) ❖ Muti, Bruscantini, Freni, Nucci, Winbergh, Ambrosian Opera Chorus, Philharmonia Orchestra (EMI) ❖

Elektra

RICHARD STRAUSS (1909)

Axe the family!

In short: A number of Greeks take an early bath.

MUSIC

The first part of this score pretty much amounts to a serious personal assault on the listener, earning its reputation as Strauss's most violent and extreme opera – even one of the singers at the première called it "a frightful din". Electra is a sort of hysterical Brünnhilde, hounding her admittedly grisly mother to death. Clytemnestra herself sings one of Strauss's most extraordinary pieces, a memorable, bitonal description of insomnia over a worming bassline – a chilling marriage of words and music. But, this being Strauss, there is another side, represented by Electra's rather more pliant sister Chrysothemis, and indeed from the moment of Orestes's return we are back in the familiar and more comfortable territory of sweeping string lines – the finale has 30 violins in four sections – and triumphant romanticism.

WORDS

By Hugo von Hofmannsthal, after Sophocles, the first of Strauss and Hofmannsthal's six collaborations.

PLOT

It is seven years since Agamemnon was dissected in his bath by his wife Clytemnestra and her new friend Aegisthus, but the household hasn't really got over it: his daughter Electra has developed something of a complex, and let her personal hygiene go into the bargain. Her sister Chrysothemis isn't quite so bad but is still in a bit of a state. Neither is all well with Clytemnestra: she is having trouble sleeping. Does Electra know any remedies for nightmares? Sure, says Electra: a sacrifice should do the trick, namely yourself, butchered in great detail by my brother Orestes. At this tricky juncture two couriers turn up with the news that Orestes has died in a high-speed chariot crash. Electra switches to plan B: she and sis will have to do the deed. Chrysothemis demurs. Plan C, then: alone. She goes to dig up the axe that did for daddy. While doing so she falls into conversation with one of the couriers, who handily turns out to be none other than Orestes.

He goes inside and sees to mum. Aegisthus appears, having just got the news about Orestes. Electra explains that the couriers are inside giving a blow-by-blow account of the sad event. Aegisthus hurries in, and gets his. Electra does a little jig and drops down dead.

STRANGE BUT TRUE

Following the Grenadier Guards' rendition of an *Elektra* medley, George V let it be known that "His Majesty does not know what the band has just played, but it is NEVER to be played again".

WHAT MAHLER THOUGHT

"We had seldom in our lives been so bored."

UNUSED WEAPONRY

One axe (after all that trouble, too).

CRUSH BAR GAMBIT

"A bit of family background: Electra's father, Agamemnon, had already killed (or tried, at least) her sister Iphigeneia. Step-father Aegisthus, also her uncle, was the product of an incestuous father-daughter relationship, and had killed her grandfather Atreus, his uncle, before doing away with Agamemnon's mistress Cassandra and their children. This family had such a well-developed death urge it is amazing they bothered to procreate at all."

RECORDINGS

❖ Solti, Nilsson, Resnik, Collier, Vienna State Opera Chorus, Vienna Philharmonic (Decca) ❖ Böhm, Borkh, Madeira, Schech, Dresden Staatskapelle (DG) ❖

L'Elisir d'Amore

GAETANO DONIZETTI (1832)

Love's liquid lunch!

In short: *A mobile wine merchant manages to shift some bin-ends of claret to a bunch of slack-jawed Basque yokels.*

MUSIC

Rossini with added pathos: it is hard to imagine him writing the droopily sweet romanza *Una furtiva lacrima*. The first of Donizetti's greatest hits – albeit his thirty-seventh opera – it is reputed to have been written in a fortnight; when told that Rossini had written *Barber of Seville* in two weeks, Donizetti remarked: "Not surprising, he's always been lazy". He shares with Mozart the ability to write simple tunes of great emotional depth, as well as a gift for characterisation: everyone in *Elisir* has unmistakeably individual music. It is a singer's showpiece, though the coloratura never holds up the action, and contains one of the greatest of *buffo* arias in Dulcamara's *Udite, o rustici*, a couple of lovely duets, and a final half-hour that is pretty close to *bel canto* perfection.

WORDS

Roundly plagiarised by Felice Romani, the Lorenzo da Ponte of his day, from a libretto by Scribe for Auber's 1831 opera *Le Philtre*.

PLOT

Act I Nemorino, a hayseed halfwit, has the hots for Adina, local beautette and gentlewoman farmer. Not surprisingly, she spurns him, making eyes instead at the sexy and moustachioed Sergeant Belcore. Nemorino buys some love potion, guaranteed to make Adina fall in love with him in 24 hours, from Dulcamara, a travelling charlatan; drinks it; gets hammered (actually, it's el cheapo plonko) and sits back, waiting for it to kick in. Adina, irritated by his sudden lack of interest in her, gets engaged to Belcore. Nemorino is unfazed until the wedding is unexpectedly brought forward to that very afternoon.

Act II *Urgently in need of more potion (to make it effective immediately, don't you see), the skint Nemorino joins Belcore's platoon and buys another bottle with the resulting king's shilling. The local girls, who have heard before anybody else (how?) that Nemorino's uncle has died leaving him a million, start making overtures to him. Everyone rather foolishly assumes the potion must be working. Adina is furious and naturally agrees to marry Nemorino on the spot. Dulcamara sells quite a lot more wine, and leaves.*

DON'T ASK
Haven't these people ever tasted wine before?

STRANGE BUT TRUE
An inveterate recycler, Donizetti used the music for Queen Elizabeth's arrival in *Il castello di Kenilworth* to announce Dulcamara's rather less grand entrance.

FIRST NIGHT BLUES
The cast contained "a German prima donna, a tenor who stammers and a *buffo* with the voice of a goat".

WHAT THE CRITICS SAID
"Perceiving it was useless to expect to hear anything of the score, I left." (Hector Berlioz, after a rowdy Milanese performance)

NOT TO BE CONFUSED WITH
Tristan and Isolde, a love-potion drama with fewer laughs.

CRUSH BAR GAMBIT
"An early example of the anti-capitalist opera, *Elisir* is the musical equivalent of Hogarth's *Gin Lane*. The peasantry is kept in subjugation with cheap intoxicants while capital, represented by the marriage of Adina and Nemorino, tends to concentrate itself in ever fewer hands. The foundations for the revolutions of 1848 are being laid."

RECORDINGS
❖ Bonynge, Sutherland, Pavarotti, Ambrosian Opera Chorus, English Chamber Orchestra (Decca) ❖ Scimone, Ricciarelli, Carreras, Turin RAI Chorus and Orchestra (Philips) ❖

Die Entführung aus dem Serail

WOLFGANG AMADEUS MOZART (1782)

Spare 'em the harem!

In short: *A botched attempt to introduce Western concubines into a Turkish harem.*

MUSIC

Entführung has the tonic effect of Rossini, although its exuberance conceals a truly Mozartian core of feeling. Jangling "Turkish" music (top of the pops in Vienna, where a Janissary band played in the Prater), folksy eastern-flavoured songs, knockabout duets and trios, and Italianate arias combine in this colourful romp that Joseph II is supposed to have said had "too many notes". The opera's heart is music of separation and reconciliation: Belmonte's yearning *O wie ängstlich*, complete with heartbeats and sighing woodwind, Constanze's heartbroken *Traurigkeit ward mir zum Lose* and defiant *Martern aller Arten*, an escapee from *opera seria*. But, really, hardly a dud number in the show.

WORDS

A very silly story of inexplicable popularity, filched from a libretto by Bretzner, bearing strong resemblances to two English plays by Isaac Bickerstaffe, set to music by Charles Dibdin. The words were provided by the universally loathed Gottlieb Stephanie, director of the new National Singspiel in Vienna, whom Mozart described as "rude, deceitful and slanderous".

PLOT

Act I *Constanze, her English maid Blonde and servant Pedrillo have carelessly allowed themselves to be captured by pirates and sold to Pasha Selim, a former Christian presently occupying a position of influence in Turkey. Constanze is now the star attraction in Selim's harem, Blonde has been given to an aged* *psychopath called Osmin and Pedrillo does the gardening. Constanze's former beau, Belmonte, comes to rescue them. He runs into Pedrillo, who succeeds in manoeuvring him into the palace.*

Act II *Blonde explains to Osmin that as an Englishwoman she is unhappy with her position as a slave and furthermore she is unwilling to submit to his sexual advances. It appears that Constanze, to date, has likewise managed to preserve her virtue, but Selim is beginning to come the heavy and threatens* force majeure. *Belmonte and Pedrillo plan their escape, Osmin is drugged and the lovers reunited.*

Act III *The escape is a disaster: Osmin's Mickey Finn wears off and he raises the alarm. In the ensuing, awkward interview it transpires that Belmonte is the son of Selim's former arch-enemy, but surprisingly Selim decides to let them all go anyway.*

WHAT THE PAPERS SAID
"Purposeless, insipid twaddle." (*Dramaturgische Blätter*, Hanover)

MOST IMPROVED PRODUCTION
Covent Garden, 1827 (English première): set in Greece, the plot included an Irish doctor, O'Callaghan; the Pasha turns out to be Constanze's brother; half the arias were re-composed by Christian Kramer, or ditched, and it was advertised as "*The Seraglio*, by the author of *Englishmen in India*, William Dimond; the music by Mozart and Kramer".

CRUSH BAR GAMBIT
"It is Mozart's anglophile manifesto, a tribute to the English inventions Freemasonry and the Enlightenment, the lodestones of Mozart's life. The Hapsburgs are invited to shake off their Spanish practices and, like Selim, adopt a more liberal form of constitutional rule as outlined by the Englishwoman Blonde."

RECORDINGS
❖ Böhm, Augér, Grist, Schreier, Moll, Leipzig Radio Chorus, Dresden Staatskapelle (DG) ❖ Mehta, Rothenberger, Grist, Wunderlich, Corena, Vienna State Opera Chorus, Vienna Philharmonic (Orfeo: live) ❖

Eugene Onegin

PYOTR ILICH TCHAIKOVSKY (1879)

Slavs to love!

In short: *A jaded Russian livens things up by shooting his best friend,
spurning a girl's love and then regretting it.*

WORDS

A selection of "lyrical scenes" from Pushkin's 5000-line Byronic verse novel,
an everyday Russian tale of meaninglessly psychotic behaviour. Shorn of
Pushkin's bitchy narrator, it becomes an emotional rendition of Tatyana's
sorry story of the impossibility of communication and the unhealthy
consequences of love. It was patched together by Tchaikovsky with help
from his brother Modest and a certain K. Shilovsky.

MUSIC

A byword, of course, for romanticism, the letter scene and loads of dancing,
but there is more to it: catchy peasant songs, wistfully passionate arias, even
a borrowed French folk tune. The tone ranges from elegiac to melancholy to
suicidal, as befits a story of missed chances and the generally awful nature
of an ineluctable fate. Although there is a six-year gap between Acts II and
III, the thing is held together by a clever interweaving of themes and keys,
and Tchaikovsky's music is so beautifully decorated and orchestrated (and
tuneful) that it is impossible not to fall for it. Lensky's pre-death musings
and Gremin's Verdian aria are the lesser-known highlights.

PLOT

Act I *Onegin's friend Lensky takes him to visit his fiancée, Olga, at her
family's place in the country. Her sister Tatyana falls for Onegin big-time, and
writes him a letter to that effect. He rather rudely gives her the brush-off.*

Act II *Nonetheless, he is invited to her birthday party, where he annoys Lensky
by flirting with Olga. A duel is arranged, on pretty scanty grounds. Onegin
shows up late and kills Lensky in an offhand sort of way.*

Act III *Six years later, Onegin runs into Tatyana at another party (in St Petersburg, this time) and decides she's not so bad after all. She points out that she is married. He leaves.*

DON'T ASK
Whatever became of Olga?

STRANGE BUT TRUE
Upon receipt of a Tatyana-esque letter from a lovestruck pupil during the composition of *Onegin*, the thoroughly homosexual Tchaikovsky foolishly failed to follow Eugene's example, and married her.
It was not a success: a couple of months later he wrote: "Death is indeed the greatest of blessings and I pray for it with all my soul."

WHAT THE CRITICS SAID
"We know butter is made from cream, but do we have to watch it being churned?" (Charles Ives)

CRUSH BAR GAMBIT
"*Onegin* is a tragedy of misread good intentions. Eugene realises Olga doesn't love Lensky and tries to set him up with the much more suitable Tatyana: hence his own selfless rejection of her. He flirts with Olga for the same reason. It's hardly his fault that Lensky and Tatyana are too stupid to get the message. As a final act of unselfishness he attempts to save Tatyana from her hellishly dull husband, but this too is thrown back in his face."

RECORDINGS
❖ Bychkov, Hvorostovsky, Focile, Shicoff, Borodina, St Petersburg Chamber Choir, Orchestre de Paris (Philips) ❖ Mackerras, Hampson, Te Kanawa, Rosenshein, Bardon, Welsh National Opera Chorus and Orchestra (EMI: in English) ❖

Falstaff

GIUSEPPE VERDI (1893)

Feeling horny!

In short: *A priapic old man takes an involuntary bath in the Thames and gets beaten up by a bunch of fairies.*

MUSIC

Verdi's last opera, and something of an oddity: short of big tunes, it is a helter-skelter ensemble piece with the orchestra playing such a starring role it seems a shame to bury them in the pit. The wordiness of the libretto is overcome by having everyone sing different words simultaneously in the kind of terrific ensembles only Mozart could do as well. Falstaff himself is one of the best-rounded (in all senses) of operatic characters: jaunty, mock-pompous, melancholic, boastful. The whole thing is closer to *Gianni Schicchi* than *Traviata*, and in common with Puccini's opera the lyrical stuff is reserved for the young lovers. Showstoppers: the Act I finale, lovers' duets alternating with quickfire, syncopated patter ensembles, ferociously hard to sing. The Windsor Great Park scene contains some wonderful Mendelssohnian fairy music.

WORDS

By Arrigo Boito out of *The Merry Wives of Windsor*, a regrettable tale of the downfall of a well-loved character, with somewhat greater prominence given to the lovers Anne and Fenton than by Shakespeare (plus a few borrowings from the other Falstaff plays).

PLOT

Act I *Falstaff's attempts to get Bardolph and Pistol to be his go-betweens with Alice Ford and Meg Page backfire when they annoyingly let Alice's husband in on the plot. Alice and Meg, too, are unhappy with the identical billets doux they receive and, with the help of Mrs Quickly, plan to teach the amorous knight a watery lesson.*

Act II *Mrs Quickly arranges a tryst between Falstaff and Alice. Mr Ford then appears in the guise of one "Fontana" (ie, Brook) to offer Jack a bag of gold if he can thaw Alice's ice as a preamble to Fontana's own seduction of her. Jack readily accepts and reveals he has already arranged the deed (which is news to Ford).*

Falstaff's subsequent attempt upon Alice is unsurprisingly interrupted when Ford pitches up; Falstaff hides in the laundry basket and gets dumped into the Thames.

Act III *Reviving himself in the pub, Jack idiotically accepts a further invitation to come (dressed as Herne the Hunter, complete with horns) to meet Alice in Windsor Great Park at midnight. Their intimacies are interrupted by the rest of the cast, disguised as fairies, who beat Falstaff up.*

Ford decides to celebrate by marrying his daughter Anne to the ghastly Dr Caius. However, since everyone is in disguise, he manages to marry Caius to Bardolph and Anne to her beloved, Fenton.

DON'T ASK
How married life turned out for Bardolph and Dr Caius.

STRANGE BUT TRUE
Arriving for the Rome première, Verdi had to hide in a toolshed at the station to escape the hysterical crowds.

CRUSH BAR GAMBIT
"The point about Falstaff, surely, is that his obvious repressed homosexuality has finally turned to psychosis. Since being jilted by Prince Hal he has lived in a solipsistic delusional state where his belly, by some weird synecdoche, has become the world, he is king, and all women are in love with him. Ironically, he is also clearly impotent: kindly ponder the implications of the word *Falstaff*."

RECORDINGS
❖ Karajan, Gobbi, Panerai, Schwarzkopf, Philharmonia Chorus and Orchestra (EMI) ❖ Toscanini, Valdengo, Guarrera, Nelli, NBC Symphony Orchestra (RCA) ❖

Faust

CHARLES GOUNOD (1859)

He sold his soul – for a song!

In short: *An elderly professor gives a young woman a pearl necklace; she dies.*

MUSIC

Too elegant to be either sublime or demonic, but annoyingly effective
even at its most reprehensible, such as Marguerite's last-ditch appeal to
the angels. Every scene has at least one good tune; the church scene with
Mephistopheles, a doom-laden choral *Dies Irae* and a crazed organist all
trying to stop Margie from praying is great theatre; and there are the
lollipops – one of opera's greatest waltz scenes, a grand march somewhere
between *Aida* and Sousa, the ballets, and of course the sparkly *Jewel Song*,
composed for the original Margie, Mme Carvalho – a relentless embellisher
of vocal parts – as a kind of damage-limitation exercise. Mephisto has a
jovial malevolence, and considerable heights of passion are reached during
the lovers' Act III duet and its ecstatic playout.

WORDS

From *Faust et Marguerite*, a piece of Goethe-lite written by Michel Carré,
and turned into a libretto by him and Jules Barbier. The Germans, poor lambs,
cannot bear to associate the opera with Goethe, and call it *Margarethe*.

PLOT

Act I *Ageing lecher Dr F, on the point of suicide, receives a surprise visit
from Mephistopheles and decides to sell him his soul in exchange for a spot of
malarkey with Marguerite, of whom Mephisto grants him a preview.*

Act II *Mephisto drops into a pub for a drink with Margie's brother Valentin
and his pals, and gets into a fight, which he wins. Then he takes Faust off to an
open-air party where he meets Margie and invites her to dance. She declines.*

Act III *Mephisto leaves a box of jewels lying around at Margie's place. This does
the trick: when she's finished admiring herself she pretty much drags Faust into bed.*

Act IV *As a result, Margie is now a single mum (and Faust being sought by the CSA). Brother Val comes back from the wars and picks a duel with Faust (now reappeared) who wins, with considerable help from Mephisto. As he checks out, Val calls down curses on his sister's head. She goes to church but her prayers are shouted down by naughty Mephisto.*

Act V *Faust and Mephisto live it up at a Walpurgis Night orgy with some high-class tarts including Cleopatra and Helen of Troy. Following this, and showing remarkable energy, they head off to visit Margie in jail, where she is due to hang in the morning for disposing of her baby. She spurns their get-out-of-jail-free card and dies. A choir of angels informs us that her soul is saved.*

Don't ask

What the heck is Mephisto doing in that church? Isn't that against the rules?

What Wagner thought

"Music for sluts."

Crush Bar gambit

"Marguerite is the objectification of Gounod's own psychosexual disorder, a peculiar blend of sickly religiosity and uncontrollable libido. Not surprisingly, given his unfortunate taste for schoolgirls, the composer associated erotic love with the demonic: Marguerite must die to expiate *his* guilt. Her murder of the child is small beer in comparison, and easily forgiven."

Recordings

❖ Plasson, Leech, Studer, van Dam, Hampson, Capitole de Toulouse Chorus and Orchestra (EMI) ❖ Rizzi, Hadley, Gasdia, Ramey, Mentzer, Agache, Welsh National Opera Chorus and Orchestra (Teldec/Warner) ❖

Fidelio

LUDWIG VAN BEETHOVEN
(1814, EVENTUALLY)

One out – all out!

In short: *Penal reform frees a number of convicted felons.*

MUSIC
After three rewrites and four overtures *Fidelio* is still a bit of a mishmash:
glorious music, but a feeble story and hobbled drama. Starting in Mozartian
buffa-Singspiel land, it is transformed in Act II as Beethoven puts his
symphonic style to work with wondrous results, particularly in the dungeon
scene. The very best bits are the Act I quartet, *Mir ist so wunderbar*, a
delicate canon with rhapsodic flutes over voices and pizzicato strings, the
yearning hope of the prisoners' chorus, *O welche Lust*, and most of Act II,
culminating in a sustained burst of overwhelming joy from the duet
O namenlose Freude to the full-throated end.

WORDS
Based on an incident in Tours during the Terror; Jean-Nicolas Bouilly, who
played the good guy on that occasion, turned it into a libretto for an opera
in 1798; Joseph Sonnleithner translated it, and it was tinkered with by
Stephan von Breuning (1806) and by Georg Friedrich Treitschke in 1814.

PLOT
Act I *We are in an 18th-century Spanish jail. Head screw Rocco lives with his
daughter Marzelline, a porter, Jaquino (who fancies her), and a new assistant
screw, Fidelio, with whom Marzelline has fallen in love. Fidelio and Marzelline
get engaged with suspicious suddenness – but not for the obvious reason:
amazingly, nobody has noticed that Fidelio is in fact a she, namely one
Leonore, wife of Mr Florestan, a prisoner presently languishing somewhere
downstairs. The prison governor Pizarro turns up with plans to do away with
Florestan, whose crime is unspecified but who Pizarro clearly doesn't care for.
He enlists Rocco's help.*

Act II *Rocco and Fidelio descend to Florestan's dungeon with instructions to dig a grave for him. Pizarro appears and explains why he's going to stab Florestan. Leonore – now in character – intervenes. Suddenly a trumpet sounds: it's the inspector of prisons, come to check for illegally-held political detainees. Pizarro tries to make a run for it (too late). The inspector, Fernando, is feeling particularly mellow and lets all the prisoners out. Everyone agrees with him that Leonore is a jolly good little wife.*

FANCY THAT

The tendency to use *Fidelio* as propaganda was aptly demonstrated by two performances in Graz: in 1933 as a pro-Nazi manifesto, and in 1945 to celebrate Austrian "liberation".

FIRST NIGHT BLUES

1805: the theatre was half-empty, and Beethoven was ditched as conductor at the last minute when the orchestra realised he was stone deaf. 1806: after delivering the score late, Beethoven accused the orchestra of "murdering my music" and withdrew the opera. 1814: he failed to provide the overture in time and had to substitute another.

WHAT THE PAPERS SAID

"Fell far below the standards to which music-lovers felt entitled."
(*Freymüthige*)

CRUSH BAR GAMBIT

"Fernando's freeing of the prisoners is a typically adolescent piece of left-wing gesture-politics. By releasing them he is putting the law-abiding Rocco, Marzelline and Jaquino out of work, probably driving them to crime into the bargain. Much better that the proven troublemaker Florestan should remain inside."

RECORDINGS

❖ Klemperer, Ludwig, Vickers, Berry, Frick, Philharmonia Chorus and Orchestra (EMI) ❖ Furtwängler, Flagstad, Patzak, Schöffler, Greindl, Vienna State Opera Chorus, Vienna Philharmonic (EMI: live at the Salzburg Festival) ❖

Die Fledermaus

JOHANN STRAUSS II (1874)

Bat hijacks ball!

In short: *A touchy lawyer's sense of humour failure nearly precipitates his friend's divorce.*

MUSIC

A conscious attempt to emulate Offenbach's Parisian successes. Though little more than a medley of waltzes and polkas, it is all done with such *élan* and some genuinely inspired musical moments that it hardly matters. It might lack Offenbach's sustained hilarity, but substitutes real Viennese *gemütlichkeit* – some might say schmaltz (plus some fairly heavy-handed humour). Strauss wrote it in six weeks and there are persistent rumours that he stole some of the music from his recently deceased brother Joseph's estate, of which he was executor. Showstoppers: the overture, a potpourri of the opera's best tunes; the mock-mournful farewell trio that turns into a jaunty polka; Adele's laughing *Mein Herr Marquis*; the Act II champagne song *Im Feuerstrom*, the show's signature tune; and Strauss's second-best-known waltz.

WORDS

A baffling mistaken-identity sex-comedy contrived by Richard Genée from *Le Réveillon* by Meilhac and Halévy, the subject of which they had swiped from a Prussian morality play, *Das Gefängnis* by Roderich Benedix. The fact that it is in three acts rather than the usual two is explained by the fact that Genée was paid 100 florins per act.

NOTE

The ball scene relies upon the notion that those present may bear a striking resemblance to one's employer, maid or wife without actually being any of those characters.

PLOT

Act I *Eisenstein has been given eight days in the slammer for an unspecified* crime and is due to hand himself over when his lawyer friend Falke tells him to postpone it till tomorrow and come to a bash chez Orlofsky, a Russian lush of dubious sexuality. Eisenstein's wife Rosalinde, thinking hubby is safely in prison, proceeds to entertain a former fancy-man, the Italian tenor Alfred. Frank, the prison governor, appears and carts Alfred off to jail, under the impression that he is Eisenstein.

Act II At the ball Eisenstein (incognito) flirts with his wife's maid (ditto), who has gatecrashed. Rosalinde shows up in a mask pretending to be a Hungarian. Eisenstein transfers his attentions to her and she steals his watch. He and Frank (yes, he's there too) become bosom chums without realising who the other is.

Act III Next morning Eisenstein presents himself at the jail. Confusion ensues. The rest of the cast also appears and Falke reveals that it has all been a jolly jape he thought up to avenge himself on Eisenstein for a childish prank (involving a bat) the latter played a while back. Multiple cases of attempted adultery are blamed on Orlofsky's champagne.

NOT MANY PEOPLE KNOW THAT

A bootleg American version (sued for breach of copyright by Strauss's widow) called *A Wonderful Night* ran for ages on Broadway in 1929, starring an expat Englishman called Archie Leach – soon to become Cary Grant.

WHAT THE CRITICS SAID

"Trite." (Eduard Hanslick)

CRUSH BAR GAMBIT

"*Fledermaus* charts the collapse of the Austro-Hungarian Empire following the debacle of Magenta. The monstrous Russo-Austrian alliance, symbolised by Orlofsky and Eisenstein, attempts to suppress Hungary – Rosalinde, of course. But thanks to their alcoholic incompetence both Hungary and Italy – the unjustly imprisoned Alfred – win their freedom."

RECORDINGS

❖ Previn, Te Kanawa, Gruberova, Brendel, Vienna State Opera Chorus and Orchestra (Philips) ❖ Karajan, Gueden, Köth, Kmentt, Vienna State Opera Chorus and Orchestra (Decca) ❖

The Flying Dutchman

RICHARD WAGNER (1843)

She lived and dived for love!

In short: *An intense Nordic seamstress takes an early bow to end the tribulations of a long-distance sailor.*

MUSIC

The overture opens with the bare fifths Wagner had associated with the supernatural since first hearing an orchestra tune up. His fourth opera has echoes of Weber, French grand and comic opera, Mendelssohn and Berlioz, all done with his customary muscularity. The action revolves about a number of rousing verse songs, beneath which Wagner creates his stormy and ghostly effects: listening to the spine-chilling Act III sailors' choruses it is easy to believe he had some kind of direct line to the demonic. A vivacious and tuneful score with the odd surprising hint of playfulness.

WORDS

The legend of the forthright sea-captain who put a word out of place attempting to round the Cape of Good Hope in a storm was already old when Heine retold it in 1834. Wagner seized upon the story, ditched Heine's ironic overtones, characteristically claimed an autobiographical inspiration and turned it into a deadly serious exposition of his peculiar views on relations between the sexes.

PLOT

Act I *Caught in a storm, a Norwegian ship anchors on the coast not far from home, where it is joined by a sinister Dutch vessel. The Norwegian captain, Daland, has a chat with the gloomy Dutch skipper, who shows great interest when Daland tells him about his daughter Senta, and offers large amounts of money to marry her.*

Act II *In Daland's house, which doubles as a sweatshop, Senta daydreams about the mythical Flying Dutchman, whose picture coincidentally hangs on her wall. This annoys her boyfriend Erik. Her father brings his new friend* home and Senta notices a striking resemblance to the picture (though nobody else seems to). She agrees to marry him. The Dutchman – for it is he – perks up at this as it means he will no longer have to wander the seas for eternity.

Act III *The Dutchman catches Senta and Erik together, jumps to conclusions, and sails off for another round-the-world trip. Senta, keen to assure him of her constancy – and also perhaps spotting a loophole in the faithful-till-death clause – leaps off a cliff. The Dutchman's ship immediately sinks and their spirits rise to heaven in a fond embrace.*

DON'T ASK
Did Daland ever get his hands on the cash?

WHAT THE PAPERS SAID
"A musical horror, a mixture concocted of bad taste and brutality in equal doses." (*Deutsche Musikzeitung*)

CRUSH BAR GAMBIT
"Senta's plan to elope with the Dutchman is a protest against the meat-based diet provided by her boyfriend, the hunter Erik. Wagner was of course a fervent vegetarian – though he was keen on herrings – and *The Flying Dutchman* is his anti-carnivore manifesto. Of course, he was also aware of the poaching of national fish stocks, and the fact that the Dutchman is dressed in Spanish costume is clearly significant."

RECORDINGS
❖ Nelsson, Balslev, Estes, Salminen, Schunk, Bayreuth Festival Chorus and Orchestra (Philips) ❖ Karajan, Vejzovic, van Dam, Mill, Hofmann, Vienna State Opera Chorus, Berlin Philharmonic (DG) ❖

La Forza del Destino

GIUSEPPE VERDI (1862, REVISED 1869)

You can run – but you can't hide!

In short: A half-Inca ex-matador with a pronounced death-wish manages involuntarily to wipe out the family of a former girlfriend.

MUSIC

This grandiose, sweeping opera is subject to many footling criticisms: sprawling, disjointed, relying on outrageous coincidence. It mixes Gothic tragedy with low comedy, its protagonists are pursued by bad luck like Greek tragedians, and their drama is brilliantly set off against low-life crowd scenes. The restless, Beethovenian theme of the showstopping overture underpins the whole opera; Alvaro and Leonora's music is soaked in yearning sixths, Carlos has a remorseless nobility, Fr Guardian great dignity and the buffo characters some catchy numbers and dance tunes. The tremendous scenes and duets make this work, even if flawed, one of breathtaking ambition and gripping intensity.

WORDS

By Francesco Maria Piave from the Duke of Rivas's *Alvaro o la fuerza del sino*, a fantastically overwrought piece of Spanish Gothic Romanticism. Verdi felt it necessary subsequently to change the bloodsoaked ending (in which Carlos and Leonora die on stage and Alvaro hurls himself off a cliff screaming anathemas on the human race).

PLOT

Act I Seville, mid-18th century. Leonora's elopement with Alvaro, a dasher of Inca origins, is forestalled by her father while she dithers. In the ensuing argument Alvaro chucks his gun on the floor, and it goes off and kills Papa, who curses them both with his dying breath. Alvaro and Leonora are separated; until their final meeting he believes she's dead and she thinks he's in Peru.

Act II 18 months later. Leonora's brother, Carlos, has sworn to kill her and Alvaro and narrowly misses running into Leonora in a pub. She goes to a nearby monastery and is given exclusive use of an isolated hermitage.

Act III Years later, in Italy, Alvaro, fighting the Austrians, rescues a fellow officer from a brawl. No prizes for guessing: it's Carlos, but since they are both incognito they swear vows of eternal friendship, etc. Alvaro is wounded in battle and asks Carlos to take care of his gear. Carlos finds a picture of Leonora among the said gear and puts two and two together. He is greatly cheered up when Alvaro recovers, since it means now he can kill him. Sadly their duel is prevented by their messmates.

Act IV Five years later. Alvaro is now a monk at Leonora's monastery (though neither knows it). Carlos tracks him down again, and provokes him to a rematch. Alvaro wins: runs to Leonora's hermitage to get somebody to confess the dying Carlos. Big surprise all round. Leonora goes to tend to Carlos, and – more surprise! – he stabs her. Alvaro feels, perhaps unreasonably, that he is finally released from all curses.

WHAT THE PAPERS SAID
"He deliberately chooses revolting subjects, because it is only these that his unreal effects can be wedded to." (*Musical Times*)

CRUSH BAR GAMBIT
"It is a drama of the unintegrated self: these characters have a pathological need to adopt different personae at every step. Alvaro, not content with disguising his Indian origin, becomes an army officer named Frederick and then a monk called Raphael; Carlos is first a student, Pereda, then Felix in the army. Leonora, even more confused than the others, has a religio-transvestite obsession."

RECORDINGS
❖ Levine, Price, Domingo, Milnes, Cossotto, Giaiotti, Bacquier, Alldis Choir, London Symphony Orchestra (RCA) ❖ Sinopoli, Plowright, Carreras, Bruson, Burchuladze, Baltsa, Ambrosian Opera Chorus, Philharmonia Orchestra (DG) ❖

Der Freischütz

Carl Maria von Weber (1821)

They supped with the Devil – with short spoons!

In short: *A man fails to shoot a pigeon despite obtaining magic bullets from the Devil; as a result, his wedding is postponed.*

Music

The original, and best, Gothic-Romantic opera, German to its socks and sandals. Weber took the Mozartian *Singspiel* – Max (tenor), Agathe (soprano) and the Hermit (bass) are musical progeny of Magic Flautists Tamino, Pamina and Sarastro – and added a rampant theatrical imagination. The 17th-century Bohemian woodland setting gives ample excuse for horns and hunting choruses, bucolic waltzes and folksy verse songs. Showstoppers: the overture, an effective scene-setter. Kaspar's jovially malicious song and aria in Act I. Agathe's big Act II aria, *Leise, leise*. The rousing Act III hunting chorus. The Wolf's Glen scene – a lighting director's dream, something entirely new, Caspar David Friedrich meets Hammer horror.

Words

Knocked up in a week by Friedrich Kind, who pinched the story from a horror compendium. *Singspiel* relies heavily on spoken dialogue of a rudimentary nature, so the characters can use their arias to expatiate at some length upon how they feel. The libretto, in common with the characters, is short on subtlety and wit, but concise. In the original story Max manages to shoot his bride, goes mad and ends his days in the nuthouse.

Plot

Act I *Max, apprentice forester, will be allowed to marry Agathe only if he can shoot a nominated pigeon, but his aim is all over the place. His colleague, Kaspar (a Bad German, often bearded) offers him some magic bullets. Max (dim, clean-shaven) agrees to meet him in the Wolf's Glen at midnight. He has clearly forgotten that Kaspar was spurned by Agathe, and might have motives.*

Act II *Agathe and her flighty cousin Ännchen are having trouble hanging a picture. In the Wolf's Glen Kaspar strikes a deal with the Black Huntsman, Samiel (ie, Old Nick): a straight swap of Max's soul for magic bullets. Kaspar and Max cook up the magic bullets. It gets windy.*

Act III *Agathe's florist carelessly substitutes a funeral wreath for her bridal bouquet. Comely youths and sturdy maidens assemble for Max's pigeon-shooting. Agathe and Kaspar are somehow obscured behind the pigeon. Max misses the pigeon and Agathe, but hits Kaspar. He dies. The local prince is keen to banish Max, but a hermit appears to plead his case. The wedding is postponed for a year as a punishment. The practice of shooting pigeons before marriage is discontinued.*

DON'T ASK
If this is Bohemia, why is it full of Germans? Where did that hermit spring from? And why is anyone interested in his opinion?

STRANGE BUT TRUE
The Vienna opening was a smash hit despite having Samiel and the Wolf's Glen removed by the censors. The Jesuits of Nîmes turned one of the tunes into a hymn to attract people to church.

CRUSH BAR GAMBIT
"This wedding should be scratched. Max's terrible aim and Agathe's bad dreams and poltergeist tendencies are obviously subconscious expressions of a profound hysterical reaction provoked by awareness of their fundamental incompatibility."

RECORDINGS
❖ Kleiber, Janowitz, Mathis, Schreier, Adam, Dresden State Opera (DG) ❖ Keilberth, Grummer, Schock, Otto, Prey, Deutsche Oper (EMI) ❖

Genoveva

ROBERT SCHUMANN (1850)

He pounced while she pined!

In short: *A returning Crusader is astonished to discover that his wife has not been unfaithful in his absence.*

MUSIC

Unjustly disparaged. It was endearingly perverse of Schumann, a specialist in songs and piano miniatures, to be so keen to write an opera, but *Genoveva* is full of lovely music. German composers were keen to produce a grand opera of German virtues (expressed here, perhaps, through Siegfried's invasion of France) to follow Weber's *Freischütz*, and the Gothic-Romantic *Genoveva* comprises folksy songs, martial choruses and a stirring Lutheran chorale linked by melodic arioso in a creditable attempt to get away from Italianate "numbers opera". Sadly the drama – which has been shaping up nicely – fizzles out somewhere in Act III and the sexual chemistry between the main characters is subatomic, but *Genoveva* is beginning to attract the attention of adventurous producers. Showstoppers: the symphonic overture; the opening chorale, also used as a frame at the end in a remarkably cinematic coup; the Golo/Genoveva duet *Wenn ich ein Vöglein wär*, as delicate as a *lied*; Margaretha's Act III magic-mirror show, with its ethereal proto-Flower Maidens; Genoveva's rapturous vision of the Virgin in Act IV.

WORDS

A mishmash of two completely different versions of the legend of St Genevieve of Brabant, a picturesque play by Ludwig Tieck and a more Byronic number by Friedrich Hebbel. The result is fairly nonsensical, but what's new? – this is opera. In the legend Genevieve ends her days wandering around the forest making friends with the animals in a fotherington-tomas sort of way.

Plot

Act I *Eighth-century Germany: Siegfried, Count Palatine, sets off to France to fight the Moors, and asks his pal Golo to look after his wife Genoveva while he is away. Bad idea: Golo has a crush on her. He enlists the help of his former nurse Margaretha, now following a new career as a witch.*

Act II *Golo attempts to rape Genoveva, without success, and spitefully arranges for a servant to be discovered in her bedroom. The servant is promptly killed and Genoveva clapped in irons.*

Act III *Margaretha poisons the wounded Siegfried in Strasbourg, but instead of dying he gets better. Golo turns up with the bad news about Genoveva. Siegfried vows to kill himself and her, but seems unsure in what order.*

Act IV *Genoveva, a prisoner, is being led through a forest; it is not entirely clear why. Nonetheless everyone seems to be able to find her without any problems: Golo appears and has another abortive crack at her, and then Margaretha, who has unexpectedly got religion and changed sides, leads Siegfried to her and reunites the pair.*

UNCONVINCING WAYS TO LEAVE YOUR LOVER
The librettist Hebbel abandoned the woman who had supported him on her meagre earnings (and borne him two sons) "for the sake of his vocation as a writer".

WHAT SHAW THOUGHT
"Pure bosh."

CRUSH BAR GAMBIT
"Golo, clearly, is in love with Siegfried rather than his wife, but, a repressed homosexual like his creator, is so emotionally bourgeois that he can express this only through projection onto the deeply wet Genoveva. It was this unintegrated psychosexual duality in the composer that eventually drove him to madness and attempted suicide."

RECORDING
❖ Harnoncourt, Ziesak, van der Walt, Gilfry, Widmer, Lipovšek, Arnold Schönberg Choir, Chamber Orchestra of Europe (Teldec) ❖

La Gioconda

AMILCARE PONCHIELLI (1876)

Grand Guignol on the Grand Canal!

In short: A Venetian busker has a bad day when her boyfriend leaves, her mother is murdered, and she kills herself rather than undergo A Fate Worse Than Death.

MUSIC

Pretty stuff with flashes of genius, and long on ironic contrast: any time somebody's hatching a particularly ghastly plot – which is usually – you can just bet a band of roistering minstrels will burst on the scene with something straight out of G&S. The dramatic decline of poor misnamed Gioconda from mere gloom to raving lunacy is of course a gift for the likes of Callas, whose rendition of her ode to suicide could gut fish at 50 paces. Other highlights include the opera's signature tune, *Voce di donna*, the tenor fave *Cielo e mar*, and *Dance of the hours* (aka Alan Sherman's *Hello Mudda, Hello Fadda*).

WORDS

Cannibalised by sometime Verdi librettist Arrigo Boito from a Victor Hugo play, *Angélo, tyran de Padoue*. A liberal use of masks leads to numerous cases of mistaken identity.

PLOT

Act I *Gioconda, a 17th-century Venetian street-singer, and her mother are waylaid by Barnaba, a secret policeman, who has designs on Gioconda. She, however, fancies Enzo, an exile who is nonetheless hanging around Venice disguised as a Croatian matelot. A crowd attempts to lynch Gioconda's mother following Barnaba's suggestion that she is a witch, but she is saved by the intervention of Laura, wife of Alvise, Barnaba's boss. Barnaba notices that there seems to be something going on between Enzo and Laura, and decides to use this to further his courtship of Gioconda.*

Act II *Barnaba spirits Laura on board Enzo's ship, ready for a quick elopement. But Gioconda, who has overheard the plot, appears, waving* *a dagger. She desists when she realises it was Laura who saved her Ma. Now Alvise, who Barnaba has cunningly tipped off, turns up with the marines. In the ensuing mayhem, everyone escapes.*

Act III *Jealous Alvise invites Laura to drink poison. Gioconda, who as usual is hiding behind a pillar, switches the poison for a Romeo-and-Juliet-style sleeping potion. Alvise throws a party which he spoils by producing Laura's apparently dead body. Enzo gatecrashes and is arrested.*

Act IV *Gioconda procures Enzo's release by promising to show Barnaba a good time. She also manages to transport the comatose Laura to her place. Enzo and Laura are reunited and set off together. Barnaba turns up with love on his mind and Gioconda finally uses her dagger – on herself. Barnaba consoles himself with the thought that at least he managed to murder her mother.*

Don't ask
Does Gioconda normally carry sleeping potion in her handbag, or is it just a lucky coincidence?

Unused weaponry
Daggers: Gioconda -v- Laura, Enzo -v- Alvise, Enzo -v- Gioconda, Gioconda -v- Barnaba; one vial of poison.

Crush Bar gambit
"The guitarist Barnaba would clearly make a good team with the singer Gioconda. Her avoidance of him, her futile pursuit of Enzo and her enthusiasm for daggers plainly indicate a morbid fear of sexual relationships, probably the result of an Electra fixation on the absent father. Suicide is the only consummation this little lady is likely to enjoy."

Recordings
❖ Votto, Callas, Cossotto, Ferraro, Cappuccilli, La Scala Chorus and Orchestra (EMI) ❖ Bartoletti, Caballé, Hodgson, Pavarotti, Ghiaurov, London Opera Chorus, National Philharmonic (Decca) ❖

Hansel and Gretel

ENGELBERT HUMPERDINCK (1893)

Something nasty in the woods!

In short: *Two truant children avoid being turned into pies, and return to a life of poverty and squalor.*

MUSIC

Giving a bunch of folk-tunes the Wagner treatment might sound like a recipe for disaster, but Humperdinck deftly pilots the reefy waters between sickening schmaltz and the terminally overblown. He treats his ingenuous little tunes and folksy dance rhythms with respect, producing something immensely German (you can hear Mendelssohn, Weber and Richard Strauss in there as well) and completely charming. The best bits are the overture and the witch's ride, the hymn-like Angels' Prayer and the children's woodland duets, particularly the ravishing beginning of Act III, which shows off Humperdinck's translucent scoring to great effect.

WORDS

Humperdinck's sister Adelheid Wette asked him to provide songs for a play she had written based on the Grimm story, and it all went so well he decided to turn it into a full-scale opera.

PLOT

Act I *Hansel and Gretel, undernourished children of the rural proletariat, are packed off to the forest to pick strawberries when their hamfisted mother manages to smash the jug of milk that was to be supper. When they've gone their father, a door-to-door broom salesman, comes home laden with food – a good broom day, apparently. He expresses surprise that Ma has sent them off to the forest, where, as is well known, a witch with peculiar dietary requirements lives. They set off to find the children.*

Act II *The children get lost and are waylaid by a Sandman who puts them to sleep. During the night they are watched over by some guardian angels (later charged with dereliction of duty).*

Act III *Having breakfasted on a gingerbread house they find in the wood, the children are then captured by its inhabitant and prepared for the oven. But by using their skill and judgment they manage to cook the witch, release a number of batter-coated children and are reunited with their parents – which might not be such a good thing.*

Don't ask
Where on earth are the social services?

Production notes
The first night had to be postponed because Gretel was ill; however this turned out quite well since it was then conducted by Richard Strauss, who became a big fan of the score's "authentic Germanness".

What the critics said
"*Ride of the Valkyries*-on-broomsticks." (Eduard Hanslick)

Not to be confused with
Please Release Me, *There Goes My Everything*, or anything else sung by the other Engelbert Humperdinck, otherwise known as Gerry Dorsey.

Crush Bar gambit
"A testament to the pernicious influence of Wagner, after whom it is impossible for the simplest fairy tale to retain its innocence, or for any family to be what it appears on the surface. Neurotic overtones are introduced by having the children's father working in the broom trade, carrying a strong hint of collusion between parents and witch."

Recordings
❖ Tate, von Otter, Bonney, Lipovšek, Schwarz, Schmidt, Hendricks, Tölz Boys' Chorus, Bavarian Radio Symphony Orchestra (EMI)
❖ Eichhorn, Moffo, Donath, Fischer-Dieskau, Berthold, Ludwig, Augér, Popp, Bavarian Radio Chorus and Orchestra (RCA) ❖

Idomeneo

WOLFGANG AMADEUS MOZART (1781)

Mayhem in the Med!

In short: A woman's search for romance on a holiday island meets with little success.

MUSIC

Gluck's influence is obvious in the use of accompanied recit and dramatic choruses, but the 24-year-old Mozart mostly takes another tack and injects huge exuberance into the old *opera seria* moulds, breaking them where it suits him. Recit and arias are bled seamlessly into one another in a nearly continuous music-drama, helped by the effortless gear-changes that Gluck could never manage, and the ensembles are entirely Mozartian. Cinematic scene-changes take place behind the music. The brilliant orchestral writing comes thanks to the Mannheim band which played at the Munich première. Showstoppers: among many, Ilia's serene *Se il padre perdei*, with lovely wind solos; the brilliantly expressive Act III quartet; Electra's pungent *accompagnato* and rage-aria *D'Oreste, d'Aiace*, worthy of the Queen of the Night.

WORDS

By the senescent Salzburg cleric Giambattista Varesco, from an earlier French libretto.

PLOT

Act I *At the seaside resort of Sidon, in Crete, young Idamantes is waiting for Papa, King Idomeneus, to return from the Trojan wars. Also present is Ilia, daughter of King Priam, who has fallen in love with Idamantes, and Electra, ditto. News arrives that Idomeneus hit a spot of weather on the way home and drowned; Idamantes goes to mope on the beach and runs into a shipwrecked mariner who turns out to be his dad after all. In all the excitement Idomeneus forgets to tell his son that he only escaped drowning by promising Neptune he would kill the first person he ran into on Crete.*

Act II *Idomeneus reckons, stupidly, that Neptune will let him off his vow if Idamantes disappears to Mycenae with Electra. No way: a nasty storm prevents their embarkation and a sea-monster comes ashore and starts causing havoc.*

Act III *Idamantes and Ilia confess their love for each other, then he shoots off to deal with the monster. Idomeneus realises he'll have to honour his vow and kill his son, who now reappears decked out for sacrifice. At the crucial moment Ilia interposes herself and Neptune finally admits defeat, with conditions: Idomeneus must resign, Idamantes must marry Ilia and take over as king. This makes everyone happy (except Electra).*

DON'T ASK

What the hell is Electra doing in Crete anyway? I thought she was supposed to be at home in Mycenae planning her mother's murder?

SUSPENSION NOTES

Travelling by coach to Munich from Salzburg for the première, Mozart had to "support myself on my hands" all the way from Wasserburg in order to "keep my arse on".

LOCAL JOURNALISM OF THE YEAR

"Libretto, music and translation are all by natives of Salzburg. The sets were masterpieces of our famous local designer Herr Lorenz Quaglio and attracted the admiration of all." (*Münchner Staatsgelehrten und vermischten Nachrichten*)

CRUSH BAR GAMBIT

"Although usually thought of as an expression of Mozart's father-fixation, *Idomeneo* is actually his way of dealing with the 'mother problem'. It is she, represented by the voracious hydra-like monster, who emasculates Idamantes. Get rid of her, and he can finally establish normal relations with both the opposite sex and his father."

RECORDINGS

❖ Gardiner, Rolfe Johnson, von Otter, McNair, Martinpelto, Robson, Monteverdi Choir, English Baroque Soloists (DG) ❖ Böhm, Ochman, Mathis, Schreier, Varady, Winkler, Leipzig Radio Chorus, Dresden State Orchestra (DG: an old-fashioned reading) ❖

Iphigeneia in Tauris

CHRISTOPH WILLIBALD VON GLUCK
(1779)

Black Sea Blues!

In short: *Some statuary is returned to Greece by unwilling Scythians.*

MUSIC

Gluck's music is so direct you have to forget Wagner, Verdi, even Mozart:
he creates his effects with the greatest economy, a single oboe line, an
uneasy bass figure, a tiny violin tremolo. It begins with a tremendous
Sturm und Drang tempest; characters express their emotions without
affectation but with considerable urgency, eschewing the recit/aria formula
of *opera seria* and substituting an accompanied arioso that blossoms into
melody somewhere between Bach and Mozart. Richard Strauss, a big fan,
paid it the compliment of rewriting it, unrecognisably.

WORDS

By Nicolas-François Guillard and the pretty magnificent Marie François Le
Blanc, Bailly du Roullet, a (male) Norman aristo, from a play by Guymond
de la Touche (and ultimately Euripides).

PLOT

Orestes, having taken care of his mum (see Elektra*), arrives in the Crimea to
retrieve a stolen statue of Diana, unaware of the rather peculiar tourism policy
in force, which requires all strangers to be killed, and also unaware that the
priestess in charge of sacrifices there is his sister Iphigeneia: he thinks she was
sacrificed years ago by Papa, Agamemnon.*

Act I *Iphigeneia has been having a startlingly accurate dream about events
back home during her prolonged absence (15 years, to date) when news arrives
that two Greeks have been caught snooping around. Thoas, the Scythian*

88

supremo, is keen to have them dispatched pronto, and Orestes and his pal Pylades (for it is they) are chucked into prison.

Act II *Orestes is quite happy to die: he has been having a tough time of it since Mycenae. Iphigeneia visits him but they fail to recognise each other, not surprising really since each thinks the other is dead.*

Act III *Iphigeneia decides to let Orestes go back to Mycenae to tell her sister Electra that she is alive and well. Orestes and Pylades have a fight about which of them should be allowed to die to save the other, which Orestes wins unfairly by saying he will kill himself rather than go back alone. Pylades sets off.*

Act IV *As he is about to be sacrificed, Orestes notes what a coincidence it is that an identical fate befell his sister Iphigeneia some time back. The ensuing moving reconciliation is interrupted by Troas and his heavies, who get into a fight with the returning Pylades and his lads. At this point Diana appears and tells the Scythians to return the statue.*

DON'T ASK
Wouldn't it have been simpler just to ask him his name?

STRANGE BUT TRUE
The administrator of the Paris opera, de Vismes, thought it would be a laugh to commission two *Iphigeneias* from Gluck and Piccinni – and then reneged on the deal to stage both. Piccinni's was eventually shown in 1780 and became known as *Iphigeneia in Champagne* owing to the prima donna's state of refreshment.

CRUSH BAR GAMBIT
"This Greek action is a classic Danzig-style provocation, designed to justify a punitive expedition against the Scythians with their funny foreign ways and lay the foundations of a fascist-imperialist state in the Crimea and the shores of the Black Sea. From this point of view, of course, it was very successful."

RECORDINGS
❖ Gardiner, Montague, Aler, Allen, Argenta, Monteverdi Chorus, Lyons Opera Orchestra (Philips) ❖ Muti, Vaness, Winbergh, Allen, La Scala (EMI) ❖

L'Italiana in Algeri

GIOACHINO ROSSINI (1813)

Run for your wife!

In short: A North African potentate realises his wife is not as bad as she seems following an encounter with an Italian women's-libber.

MUSIC

Should be prescribed instead of Prozac, it's such heartening stuff without any apparent side-effects except harmless addiction. Rossini is the despair of harder-working composers, who mutter at the effortless gold he spins from the seeming dross of musical clichés – but then most of them, from overture to patter song to thumping stretta, are his own inventions, and it is in this work, his eleventh opera and first *buffa* hit, that the structures of Italian opera for the next generation begin to crystallise. Pointless to talk of highlights in this score: just get carried away by the rhythm, delirious invention, incendiary coloratura, most insane first act climax and happiest finale on record.

WORDS

A second-hand libretto (by Angelo Anelli) set by Rossini in a hurry when the Teatro San Benedetto in Venice needed an opera at short notice (27 days). A rarity – a genuinely funny piece of *commedia dell'arte*-inspired lunacy.

PLOT

Act I *Mustafa, Bey of Algiers, is keen to dump his wife Elvira and taste some Italian charms instead, to which end he commissions his head pirate, Haly, to hijack an Italian ship. Elvira will be married off to Lindoro, an Italian captive, who is himself bemoaning his lost beloved, Isabella. Haly moves pretty smartly and captures a ship among whose passengers are the same Isabella, en route to*

Galicia to look for Lindoro, and her elderly travelling companion Taddeo, whom she has promised to marry if she can't find Lindoro.

Lindoro and Elvira, due to embark for Italy, pop in to say goodbye to Mustafa, who is just making his move on Isabella, who insists that Lindoro remain as her slave. Considerable confusion follows.

Act II *Isabella plans their escape, leading Mustafa on all the while. Lindoro and Taddeo tell him that to get anywhere he must become the ideal husband, a Pappataci, who does nothing but eat and sleep. Mustafa, an idiot, is very pleased with his new status, but carries out his duties so well that all the Italians escape, and Mustafa decides he's better off with Elvira than an Italian rompipalle.*

COMPOSER'S VIEW
"I thought when they heard it the Venetians would decide I was crazy – but it turns out they are even crazier…"

BLUE PENCIL NOTES
The Papal censor insisted on changing the aria *Pensa alla patria* to *Pensa alla sposa* ("think of your wife"), but failed to notice the subversive *Marseillaise* quotation just before it. The opera was also retitled *The happy shipwreck* in case anyone had any untoward thoughts about Italian unity.

NOT TO BE CONFUSED WITH
Il Turco in Italia, Rossini's next effort, boycotted by the audience at La Scala, who assumed (wrongly) he was taking the mickey by rehashing both plot and music.

CRUSH BAR GAMBIT
"Rossini's anti-globalisation manifesto makes the often overlooked point that opposition to cultural imperialism – represented by the importation of trendy Italian marital standards – is a two-way street. It is up to Mustafa, a sucker for Eurotrash, to reassert his cultural identity and take pride in his native heritage."

RECORDINGS
❖ Abbado, Baltsa, Raimondi, Lopardo, Vienna State Opera Chorus, Vienna Philharmonic (DG) ❖ Scimone, Horne, Palacio, Ramey, Prague Philharmonic Chorus, Solisti Veneti (Erato/Warner) ❖

Jenůfa

LEOŠ JANÁČEK (1904)

Trouble a't'mill!

In short: *A Moravian peasant cancels her wedding with one cousin, only to marry another.*

MUSIC
Janáček's first operatic success. His music weds a novel form of speech-song (with a miraculous ability to catch particular tones of voice) with an orchestral style based on short phrases and a tendency to ignore traditional rules of harmonic progression, ideal material with which to construct the neurotic atmosphere that pervades much of *Jenůfa*. But he was also a sucker for the soprano voice, and the vocal line often blossoms into gorgeous phrases over a sustained accompaniment of strings, evoking the serene forgiveness that is the opera's true message. Tension is also relieved with folksy episodes of singing and dancing, particularly a rumbustious *odzemek* in Act I and some jaunty bridesmaids in Act III.

WORDS
Janáček's own adaptation of Gabriela Preissová's play *Her Step-daughter*, which annoyed romantics with its realism and realists because of its religious overtones.

PLOT
Act I *Jenůfa, carelessly impregnated by her cousin, local mill-owner Števa, is keen to marry him asap; but her stepmother (a churchwarden, known as Kostelnička), ignorant of the forthcoming Happy Event, makes them put off the wedding for a year while Steve lays off the booze. Steve's half-brother Laca, who also has a thing about Jen, reckons this might put him in with a chance, but Jen tells him to get lost. He goes crazy and carves up her face with his knife.*

Act II *Kostelnička has discovered the truth and is trying to keep the (recently born) baby a secret by pretending Jen's in Vienna. Steve has got engaged to the* *mayor's daughter. Laca is still hanging around, and Kostelnička tells him about the baby, hurriedly adding that it's dead when he suddenly goes cool on the idea of marrying Jen. Wish being father to the thought, she drugs Jen, grabs the baby and heads off to drown it under the ice in the river, then tells Jen it died while she was asleep. Laca and Jen make plans to marry, and Kostelnička begins to get panic attacks.*

Act III *Just as Laca and Jen are about to set off to get married there is a commotion as a baby's body is discovered (ice now thawed). Kostelnička confesses all and is hauled off, not before Jen has forgiven her. Laca says he'll stick around anyway.*

DON'T ASK
Mightn't it be a better idea to marry outside this particular family?

WHAT THE PAPERS SAID
"Obviously the work of a man only a cut above the amateur."
(*New York Evening Post*)

CAUTIONARY NOTE
In 1887 Janáček wrote a review of an opera by Karel Kovařovic praising the composer's genius – "to provoke deafness". Big mistake: Kovařovic became music director of the National Theatre in Prague and rejected *Jenůfa* eight times before its first performance there in 1916, when he also insisted on editing and rescoring it (thereby getting royalties for life).

CRUSH BAR GAMBIT
"Števa represents the German-speaking robber-capitalists who 'inherited' the means of production from their rightful Czech owners, namely Laca, and treated their employees as feudal serfs, first night rights included. They also had political power sewn up, as seen in Števa's liaison with the mayor's daughter."

RECORDING
❖ Mackerras, Söderström, Randová, Dvorský, Ochman,
Vienna Philharmonic (Decca) ❖

Julius Caesar

GEORGE FRIDERIC HANDEL (1724)

Nile desperandum!

In short: *Family strife in Egypt leads to an imperialist takeover.*

MUSIC

Despite its extreme length (best part of four hours), JC is the most dramatic of *opere serie*. Ostensibly a story of historical feuds, it is actually mostly concerned with the tricky early moments in Julius and Cleopatra's affair. Her arias in particular (they each have eight) constitute a character study of great depth, from flighty sex-bomb via seductress, vulnerable lover and bereft broken-heart to her eventual triumph. Perhaps the best are *Se pietà*, a Bach-like invocation of striking unhappiness; *Piangerò*, a major-key threnody over a Purcellian falling bassline; *V'adoro, pupille*, her seduction saraband; Caesar's bouncy *Va tacito*, really an excuse for the star castrato Senesino to duel with a French horn; and the wilting *siciliano* duet *Son nata a lagrimar* between Cornelia and Sextus.

WORDS

By Nicola Haym, based on a libretto by Bussani already used for two operas in Italy.

PLOT

Act I *Caesar arrives in Egypt looking forward to the away leg of his match with Pompey, and is understandably miffed when local king Ptolemy, attempting to ingratiate himself, presents him with Pompey's head on a plate. Pompey's widow Cornelia tries unsuccessfully to stab herself, and her son Sextus tells Ptolemy he's going to kill him, whereupon he and Cornelia are immediately arrested.*

Act II *Ptolemy's sister Cleopatra, who is trying to grab the throne, puts on a bit of a show (disguised as one Lydia) for Caesar, which has the desired effect of making him fall in love with her. Meanwhile Ptolemy and his henchman Achilla are competing for the affections of Cornelia, who flunks another* suicide attempt, which this time consists of throwing herself to the royal lions. Caesar is getting on nicely with Cleo (now back in character) when an assassination squad arrives. He dives into the harbour and is presumed drowned. Ptolemy tries to rape Cornelia, and now it's Sextus's turn to try suicide (evisceration-type), without success.

Act III There is a battle, which Ptolemy wins despite having Achilla switch sides at the last minute. To general surprise Caesar emerges from the harbour, towels himself down and heads off to find Cleo, now a prisoner. Sextus finally manages to kill Ptolemy, who is having a last shot at raping Cornelia.

PRODUCTION BLUES

Feckless stage-hands forgot to change the side-scenes: "… I must own I was not a little astonished to see a well-dressed young Fellow, in a full bottom'd Wigg, appear in the midst of the Sea, & without any visible Concern taking Snuff." (*The Spectator*)

WHAT THE CRITICS THOUGHT

"It was the first Entertainment of this Nature that I ever saw, and will I hope be the last." (John Byrom)

CRUSH BAR GAMBIT

"*Julius Caesar* is Handel's *Fidelio*, a hymn to wedded love based on the premise that extra-marital sex is a blood sport: it is no accident that the only character who in the long run avoids a sticky end is Cornelia, the faithful if bereaved wife. Cleo of course was married to Ptolemy as well as being his sister, and Caesar had Calpurnia, his third wife, back in Rome."

RECORDINGS

❖ Jacobs, Larmore, Schlick, Fink, Rorholm, Ragin, Concerto Köln (Harmonia Mundi) ❖ Mackerras, Jones, Baker, Walker, Bowman, Tomlinson, ENO Chorus and Orchestra (Chandos: in English) ❖

Katya Kabanova

Leoš Janáček (1921)

Tales from the riverbank – Russian style!

In short: *A highly-strung girl has an affair while her husband is off on business, tells everyone about it, then drowns herself in the Volga.*

MUSIC

Modernish, but not scary: anyone who can handle Mahler can cope with this. Janáček's music is absolutely his own, but has echoes of everything from late Romanticism to Bartók. Scenes are built out of short themes that are varied, intertwined and developed to huge dramatic effect. Each character also has a motif or musical signature, Katya's being plangent strings, harp and viola d'amore. Janáček can produce climaxes to match Puccini, and has a way of conjuring chords and harmonic progressions out of chaos that gives you goose-pimples. It is Katya's show: a real star role, but she needs to be up to it. Showstoppers: Act I: Katya confesses her longings to Varvara. An ecstatic piece with luscious orchestration, coming to an amazing resolution like something out of Strauss's last songs. The double love scene: Varvara and Kudryash serenade each other folksily while Katya and Boris soar in romantic abandon. Act III: after a last, Puccinian, love scene, Katya, as mad as Ophelia, sings a sweet farewell and takes the plunge.

WORDS

A Czech translation of Alexander Ostrovsky's play about the horrors of provincial Russian life, *The Storm*. Janáček was in (unrequited) love with a married woman 40 years his junior, so the theme of Katya's adulterous affair was of some considerable interest to him, if only as wish-fulfilment.

PLOT

Act I Katya lives with her feckless drunk of a husband, Tikhon, and her mother-in-law Kabanikha, a psychotic Russian brute from central casting. Tikhon is about to go off on a business trip, and Katya fears the worst because she has fallen in love (from a distance) with Boris – who is staying nearby with his uncle Dikoy, another thug – and has a good idea how things will turn out with Tikhon away. She swears to Tikhon that she won't talk to any young men in his absence, failing which she wishes to die unshriven without seeing her parents again – which, of course, is exactly what is going to happen.

Act II *Varvara, Kabanikha's foster-daughter, arranges to meet her beau Kudryash by the river at night, and for Katya to meet Boris. Katya is horrified by the prospect but just can't help herself. She meets Boris. They declare their love.*

Act III *A storm brews. Tikhon returns unexpectedly. Katya, hysterical, tells Tikhon and Kabanikha she has spent the last ten nights with Boris, and runs off into the storm. Then she wonders why she spilt the beans: so do we. She meets Boris one last time, then throws herself into the Volga (which has itself begun to sing, spookily). Kabanikha crows in glee.*

CRUSH BAR GAMBIT

"Of course, Katya's fatal confusion between the sex urge and the death urge is hardly surprising when you consider the hopeless *zugzwang* she's in, crushed between the suffocating, ur-Slavic matriarchy represented by Kabanikha and the unregainable erotic freedom of the unmarried Varvara."

RECORDING

❖ Mackerras, Söderström, Dvorský, Kniplová, Vienna State Opera, Vienna Philharmonic (Decca) ❖

Khovanschina

MODEST MUSORGSKY (1880)

Russian to destruction!

*In short: Peter the Great becomes Tsar despite considerable efforts to stop him.
Nearly everybody dies.*

MUSIC
Typified by the contrast between the gentle pastoral prelude and the
first scene where the Moscow police proudly discuss the previous day's
atrocities. The ill-fated Old Believers have a sonorous dignity; everyone
else indulges the national sports of alcohol, murder, rape, folk-singing and
bewailing the state of Russia at the drop of a hat. It is a very chatty opera
(though nobody is listening to anyone else) underpinned by music ranging
from lyrical to violent, often modal. Left in scattered pieces at his untimely
alcoholic death by the composer, the score was variously put together and
orchestrated by Rimsky-Korsakov and, later, Shostakovich – the version
usually heard today.

WORDS
Various scenes of desultory squabbling based on dynastic plots, none
of which are explained, cobbled together by Musorgsky from numerous
sources including his own imagination. Complicated by the fact that
censorship forbade the depiction of the two main protagonists, Peter and
Sophia.

BACKGROUND
The title means "The Khovansky Affair". Mr K is head of the Streltsy,
an SS-style private army with the Moscow policing franchise. He is keen to
prevent Peter becoming Tsar, a job he fancies himself. Equally anti-Peter
are the Old Believers, a strongly pro-beard religious group headed by one
Dosifey. Prince Golitsyn, broadly anti-beard, is in favour of westernisation.
Shaklovity, a boyar, has his own non-beardist agenda which places him in
conflict with all the above.

PLOT

Act I *Khovansky's son Andrei tries to rape a German girl but is prevented by Marfa, his old flame and an Old Believer, too. Shaklovity (new lover of the regent Sophia, as we are not told) composes an anonymous denunciation of the Khovansky family in traditional style.*

Act II *Golitsyn – ex-lover of Sophia – hears bad news about his future from Marfa, moonlighting as a fortune-teller. He tries to have her killed, unsuccessfully. Then he has a pointless argument with Khovansky and Dosifey about Russia's future.*

Act III *The Streltsy hear that Peter's troops are coming to get them.*

Act IV *Khovansky is killed while being entertained by his harem: Shaklovity is responsible. Golitsyn is sent into exile and the Streltsy are arrested, but pardoned just before they get their heads chopped off. (Don't panic, Peter will later execute two thousand of them on Red Square.)*

Act V *The Old Believers decide the best thing is to commit mass suicide by combustion; Marfa persuades Andrei to join her in the bonfire.*

DON'T ASK

If everyone is so concerned about Russia's future, why don't they
do something about it?

STRANGE BUT TRUE

Sophia, the regent with all the lovers, was described as "immensely fat, with a head as large as a bushel, hairs on her face and tumours on her legs".

CRUSH BAR GAMBIT

"*Khovanschina* is basically a catalogue of the various types of doom available to Russians. The general populace enjoys being brutalised by the Streltsy. Other possibilities include being murdered by your supposed allies, falling victim to mass execution or mass suicide. In the circumstances Musorgsky's own alcoholism and madness seem a sensible choice."

RECORDINGS

❖ Abbado, Haugland, Lipovšek, Atlantov, Burchuladze, Vienna State Opera (DG) ❖ Gergiev, Minzhilkiev, Borodina, Pluzhnikov, Okhotnikov, Kirov Opera (Philips) ❖

Lady Macbeth of Mtsensk

DMITRI SHOSTAKOVICH (1934)

Dial Lady M for murder!

In short: Two Russians are too busy having sex to be bothered to dispose of a body properly, with foreseeable consequences.

MUSIC

A raucous score that veers between lyricism, tragedy and low farce, breaking out occasionally into brassy, syncopated show-tunes. Parts are in dubious taste, notably the explicit Act I sex-scene complete with farting, post-coital trombones. Katerina's music, snaky melodies woven around with solo woodwind lines, depicts her, ironically, as the only decent character in a world of random brutality and betrayal, surrounded by moronic psychopaths: "a quiet Russian family who beat and poison one another … a modest picture drawn from nature." The final act reaches a climax of wrenching despair. Stalin saw it in January 1936 and was not amused; the show was banned.

WORDS

From an 1865 story by Nikolai Leskov about the ghastliness of life in the Russian provinces (didn't they have anything else to write about?). The libretto, by Sasha Preis, omits one superfluous murder.

PLOT

Act I *Katerina takes advantage of her husband Zinovy's absence to have a fling with a new handyman, Sergei. They are caught by Zinovy's father Boris, who also wouldn't be averse to "comforting" Katerina while Zinovy is away. He gives Sergei a flogging, and Katerina gives Boris some mushrooms sautéed with rat poison. He dies.*

Act II *Zinovy returns, discovers Sergei under Katerina's bed and is strangled for his trouble. They carelessly shove his body in the cellar and decide to marry, like the good Christian folk they are.*

Act III *The wedding day. Zinovy's by now rather smelly corpse is discovered by a drunk peasant on a vodka hunt. Showing remarkable social awareness he goes to the police, who are coincidentally trying to think up a pretext to get to the wedding party. They appear, Katerina hysterically gives herself up, and she and Sergei are arrested.*

Act IV *En route – on foot – to Siberia, Sergei takes a shine to another prisoner, Sonyetka, and tricks Katerina out of a pair of stockings which he trades with the former for a quickie. Katerina pushes Sonyetka off a bridge, then jumps into the river herself. They are both poor swimmers, and drown.*

LIGHT-HANDED CRITICISM – BEFORE STALIN'S VISIT
"A result of the general success of the Party's correct policy towards all sections of the country's cultural life … our culture has now surpassed the most advanced capitalist culture." (*Sovietskaya Muzyka*, 1934)

… AND AFTER
"Leftist bedlam instead of human music … petty-bourgeois clowning … tickles the perverted tastes of the bourgeois …" (*Pravda*, 1936)

WHAT STRAVINSKY THOUGHT
"Lamentably provincial."

NOT TO BE CONFUSED WITH
Turgenev's story *Hamlet of Schigrovsk*.

STRANGE BUT TRUE
The première was part of the seventeenth Party Congress's drive to keep pace with production quotas established for the coal-miners of the Donbass.

CRUSH BAR GAMBIT
"Stalin was obviously a fairly astute critic, seeing in Sergei a satire on his ideal *homo sovieticus* to whom betrayal is first nature. He also saw unwelcome parallels between the parody of the police arresting socialists with his own plans for the Old Bolsheviks, shortly to be exterminated *en masse*."

RECORDING
❖ Rostropovich, Vishnevskaya, Gedda, London Philharmonic
Orchestra (EMI) ❖

Lakmé

LEO DELIBES (1883)

Saying it with flowers!

In short: *Imperialist English pigs dispose of an Indian goddess.*

MUSIC

So long as you don't come to *Lakmé* with wildly unrealistic expectations,
there's plenty to enjoy – and not just the Flower Duet and Bell Song.
A vehicle for star coloratura soprano and tenor, it is full of the exoticism of
uncertain provenance of which the French were inordinately fond in the
late 19th century: they pretty much used the same idiom for anything from
Morocco to Indo-China, via ancient Palestine. *Lakmé* is stuffed with good
tunes, even if some of them sound closer to boulevardier's *chanson* than
Grand Opera, and is orchestrated in a light-fingered, fey manner, all muted
violin arpeggios, high-lying wind chords and the lachrymose tones of cor
anglais and clarinet. The English quintet are provided with jaunty
ensembles straight out of a G&S tea-party.

WORDS

By Edmond Gondinet and Philippe Gille, based on the autobiographical
novel *Rarahu*, or *The Marriage of Loti*, by Julien Viaud, aka Pierre Loti,
the man also responsible for *Madame Chrysanthème*, a *Butterfly*-like tale
set to music by Messager. Loti's writings have been described as exhibiting
a "gross misunderstanding" of the cultures he encountered: *Lakmé* is
certainly no exception, even if it was originally set in Tahiti. The model for
Lakmé, Rarahu, apparently did not do herself in when Loti left but ended
her days a nymphomaniac alcoholic with an insatiable appetite for passing
French sailors.

PLOT

Act I *Surprisingly enough, we are in the Raj, where naughty Brahmin*
Nilakantha has failed to understand the advantages of British rule and is
fomenting rebellion. Furthermore, he has made his daughter Lakmé a goddess.

While the Indians are away from their nice secret garden and temple a quintet of imperialist English – two officers, their girlfriends and a comic governess – wander in and take liberties with the place. One of them, Gerald, remains behind when the others leave, runs into Lakmé and inevitably falls in love with her. Her father finds out and decides to kill whoever is responsible.

Act II *At a street party in the local town Nilakantha uses Lakmé as bait to catch Gerald, who appears on cue when she starts singing. He gets stabbed by Nilakantha's hitmen.*

Act III *Lakmé rescues Gerald and takes him off to convalesce in the jungle. He is tracked down by brother officer Frederick who persuades him to return to the regiment, which is just off to do some biffing. Lakmé is pretty unhappy about this and eats a datura flower (bad: poisonous). As she's dying Nilakantha turns up but has to be nice to Gerald who has used the time profitably to become his son-in-law.*

FANCY THAT

Loti's amorous adventures also took him to Istanbul, where you can still enjoy a sundowner at the Café Pierre Loti.

CRUSH BAR GAMBIT

"Gerald's highly inappropriate behaviour exposes the nature of French imperialism as unleashed libido. From North Africa to Polynesia, from Delacroix to Gide, the empire was more a pathological dominatory fantasy than a physical phenomenon, expressed in a fever of erotic frenzy, albeit not generally directed towards the young ladies of the colonies. The anglophobia of *Lakmé* is a classic illustration of subconscious projection and guilt-transference."

RECORDINGS
❖ Bonynge, Sutherland, Vanzo, Bacquier, Monte Carlo Opera Chorus and Orchestra (Decca) ❖ Plasson, Dessay, Kunde, van Dam, Capitole de Toulouse Chorus and Orchestra (EMI) ❖

Lucia di Lammermoor

GAETANO DONIZETTI (1835)

Lucy loses it!

In short: *Scottish wedding: three dead.*

MUSIC

Donizetti never made any great claims for himself, but *Lucia* is a master-piece of Gothic tragedy, demonstrating that his effortless *bel canto* could convey high emotion as well as amiable comedy. Of course the mad scene is known for its fireworks, but it is the way he uses coloratura to express Lucy's gradual unhingeing that is the stroke of genius. Given the generally jaunty accompaniments, it is extraordinary how Donizetti's vocal lines manage to express these baroque passions, Henry's distinctly intemperate anger, Edgar's unquenchable ardour; nowhere better demonstrated than the overwrought Act II sextet, underpinned by a bouncy dance-tune. Other highlights are Lucy's sortita, *Regnava nel silenzio*, complete with a lovely harp solo (originally planned for glass harmonica, which would have been spooky), and Edgar's final cavatina, *Tu che a Dio*, a tuneful piece of authentically febrile despair.

WORDS

Walter Scott was all the rage in Europe and it was the matter of a moment for jobbing librettist Salvatore Cammarano to fillet *The Bride of Lammermoor*.

PLOT

Scotland, about 1689. Edgar Ravenswood, former nob and Jacobite, has been dispossessed by parvenu Henry Ashton in the Williamite wars. It rankles: in fact they both spend large amounts of their time swearing to kill one another. Henry, for political reasons, wants his sister Lucy to marry Arthur, Lord Bucklaw. But she has other ideas …

Act I ... *namely, to marry Edgar, who recently whipped her out of the path of a rampaging bull, causing her to fall in love with him. Edgar now finds it expedient to go to France, but before he leaves they exchange vows of eternal love, rings, etc.*

Act II *Lucy, always rather glum, is now in a permanent decline. Henry forges a letter casting doubt on Edgar's fidelity. Then he produces Arthur and hustles Lucy through the gloomiest wedding in history. Who should turn up, even before the ink is dry, but Edgar, hot off the ferry. He creates a scene, returns his ring, and leaves, swearing.*

Act III *Later that evening Henry seeks Edgar out and taunts him with visions of Lucy making whoopee with Arthur. As intended, this leads to a challenge. Back at the castle things have perked up, but the mood soon passes when it transpires that the wedding night isn't going too smoothly, and actually Lucy has just skewered Arthur in the bedroom. She appears, completely off her rocker. End of party. Edgar, waiting patiently for his duel, is apprised of the latest facts. A bell begins to toll: Lucy is dead. He kills himself.*

NOT MANY PEOPLE KNOW THAT

In Parma, in 1837, the ladies' chorus was arrested for wearing red and green ribbons, construed by the Austrian plod as a reference to the Napoleonic tricolour.

CRUSH BAR GAMBIT

"*Lucia* is Donizetti's revenge on the Neapolitan censor, who banned *Maria Stuarda* in 1834 for its Protestant propaganda. The dispossession of the Stuarts that is behind *Lucia* conveys the same message to the Hapsburgs rather more subtly: forget about the divine right of kings, history is on our side ..."

RECORDINGS

❖ Bonynge, Sutherland, Pavarotti, Milnes, Ghiaurov, Royal Opera House Chorus and Orchestra (Decca) ❖ Karajan, Callas, di Stefano, Panerai, Zaccaria, La Scala (EMI: live, with cuts) ❖

Macbeth

GIUSEPPE VERDI (1847, REVISED 1865)

She mocked him to murder – and they slept no more!

In short: Macbeth receives assurances that he will become king of Scotland, but his wife is keen to speed up the process. They both go mad, and die.

MUSIC

The best of early Verdi. The witches are tunefully spiteful, Lady Macbeth spiky and dotted, and Macbeth broods with melodic anguish. Clever orchestration heightens the drama, and the chromatic choral writing is on the way to the much later *Requiem*. The first two acts in particular rise to splendidly histrionic extended finales, with the chorus taking a starring, noisy role. Lady M – with "the voice of a she-devil" – was a perfect part for Callas. Showstoppers: the murder scene, complete with hooting owlets, is high on horror (Macbeth) and contempt (Lady M), and leads, via a tremendous thumping on the castle door straight out of *Don Giovanni*, to the first finale, a thunderous affair crying for vengeance. Banquo's ghost brings out the best of Lady M's hysterical jollity and Macbeth's wild-eyed madness. Marvellous lunacy from the pair of them at the end of Act III.

WORDS

Verdi sent a synopsis of the play to his librettist Piave with a plea that they make "something extraordinary" out of "one of mankind's greatest creations". Piave's version successfully compresses the drama into a little over two hours.

PLOT

Act I Macbeth and Banquo are out walking when they receive various surprising items of news from 18 old ladies. Macbeth notes that two prophecies have already come true but suspects the third might need a helping hand. His wife agrees. As it happens, King Duncan is just visiting, so they kill him. Macbeth wonders whether this was a mistake, but his wife pooh-poohs the idea.

Act II *The now royal couple decide that Banquo is surplus to requirements, and commission his murder. His ghost then appears at a party, and spoils it.*

Act III *Macbeth meets the 18 old ladies again and receives mixed reports concerning his future. He decides that, just in case, he'd better get rid of Macduff, but fails.*

Act IV *Scotland is plunged into war as Duncan's son comes to avenge his father. Lady Macbeth dies, and Macbeth is killed by Macduff, who is exempt from prophecies.*

DON'T ASK
Why on earth is King Duncan's arrival announced by a lilting *siciliano*?

STRANGE BUT TRUE
Improbably adopted by Italian unificationists, who, when forbidden to throw red and green bouquets to the singers in Venice by the Austrian authorities, threw them instead in Austrian colours, yellow and black, for the pleasure of seeing the singers scorn to pick them up. Callas refused to sing Lady Macbeth at the Met immediately before Violetta (*La Traviata*), remarking: "My voice is not an elevator."

CRUSH BAR GAMBIT
"Verdi's Macbeths become operatic outsiders by sublimating libido into ambition, and put themselves beyond the protection of those tutelary deities who watch over lovers. The *acte gratuit* of this existential drama is not the murder but the voluntary unsexing of the protagonists."

RECORDINGS
❖ de Sabata, Mascherini, Callas, Tajo, Penno, La Scala (EMI)
❖ Leinsdorf, Warren, Rysanek, Hines, Bergonzi, Metropolitan Chorus and Orchestra (RCA) ❖

Madama Butterfly

GIACOMO PUCCINI (1904)

Her hopes went up – in a puff of smoke!

In short: Ethnically disadvantaged teenage single mum kills herself when imperialist father gets custody of the kid.

MUSIC

Puccini in full flow, the main difference from *Tosca* and *Bohème* being a random use of Japanesery like the pentatonic scale. *Butterfly* contains Puccini's most passionate music (the love duet), some of the most lyrical (Butterfly's arrival, the Humming Chorus, the Flower Duet), his best-known soprano aria (*Un bel dì*), one of the most effective dramatic moments (when Butterfly produces her baby) and perhaps the most hair-raising climax. All this plus the experience – previously available only to lachrymose Americans – of *The Star-Spangled Banner* bringing a tear to your eye. It can also be rather unengaging until Butterfly turns from wearisome airhead to tragic heroine towards the end.

WORDS

By Puccini's A-Team, Giacosa and Illica, from a play by David Belasco from a short story by John Luther Long, and a great improvement on both, with the Americans caricatured quite as much as the Japanese.

PLOT

Act I *Lieutenant Pinkerton is shown around his new Nagasaki house by Goro, estate agent, marriage broker and creep. Pinkerton tells the American consul, Sharpless, that he has contracted for house and wife on the same terms: ie a 999-year lease with a get-out clause every month. Sharpless disapproves, particularly when the dim, trusting 15-year-old Cho-Cho-San, aka Butterfly, appears (though he is not above asking whether she has any sisters). She and Pinkerton get married despite representations from an angry uncle.*

Act II *Three years later. Pinkerton left shortly after the marriage with promises to return "when the robins nest". Sharpless comes to visit bearing his Dear John letter but chickens out from revealing its contents when Butterfly produces her blue-eyed baby.*

Butterfly spots Pinkerton's gunboat arriving in the harbour and sits up all night waiting for him; he finally appears when she's fallen asleep. He has come to claim the child, and thoughtfully brought with him his new, American, wife. Mrs P enters negotiations with Butterfly's maid Suzuki and subsequently with Butterfly. She, finding it all too much, slices her throat.

STRANGE BUT TRUE
Benjamin Franklin Pinkerton is referred to throughout as F.B. Pinkerton because in the original libretto his name, for some reason, was Sir Francis Blummy Pinkerton.

NOT TO BE CONFUSED WITH
Messager's 1893 opera *Madame Chrysanthème*, an improbable tale of a naval officer's temporary marriage to a geisha.

CRUSH BAR GAMBIT
"Far from being the anti-American diatribe it is often considered, *Butterfly* is in fact an astonishingly prophetic parable about the Japanese love affair with the USA and the destructive effects of projection. Cho-Cho-San's hysterical schizophrenia can only be resolved by complete identification with The Other. Her suicide prefigures Hiroshima."

RECORDINGS
❖ Karajan, Freni, Pavarotti, Vienna Philharmonic, Vienna State Opera Chorus (Decca) ❖ Karajan, Callas, Gedda, La Scala (EMI) ❖

The Magic Flute

WOLFGANG AMADEUS MOZART (1791)

Love on the level!

In short: *A royal hostage acquires a taste for captivity, and gets married.*

MUSIC:

Mozart's strangest opera and his last, premiered two months before he died. This astonishing music ("the only opera in existence that might conceivably have been written by God", according to Neville Cardus) completely transcends the libretto's trite moralising about universal brotherhood and wedded love. It must have been a bit of a surprise for the first night audience, expecting a vaudeville of songs and patter with tunes to match: certainly the *Flute* has its folksy bits – ie, Papageno – but it also contains a stunning *opera seria* revenge aria with stratospheric coloratura (the grave-yard of many an aspiring soprano), a Lutheran chorale, a lilting Handelian lament, and some pretty solemn Masonic-ritual music; all this plus something never heard before or since, that of Mozart's three boys intoning sounds from another world. It is funny, tragic, moving and uplifting: only the hardest of hearts can remain unmelted.

WORDS

A mixture of fairy-tale, myth and Masonic allegory by travelling showman Emanuel Schikaneder with help from his troupe, including one Karl Giesecke, who later became Professor of Mineralogy at Trinity College, Dublin and lived as an Eskimo in Greenland. Sources include *Lulu, oder die Zauberflöte* by A.J. Liebeskind and *Sethos* by Abbé Jean Terrasson.

PLOT

Act I *Tamino, a Japanese (or Javanese, or Ruritanian, depending on your source) prince on holiday (apparently) in Egypt, is rescued from a hungry snake by some female employees of a local queen and sent on a mission to rescue the queen's kidnapped daughter, Pamina. In the company of Papageno (a man who imprisons small birds for a living) and handily equipped with a magic flute and* *glockenspiel, he attempts to infiltrate the castle where Pamina is being held hostage, and gets arrested. In a surprise move he decides to join the shadowy, sexist outfit that organised the kidnapping.*

Act II *Tamino undergoes some not very rigorous initiation and eventually gets to marry Pamina. Papageno is similarly provided with a girlfriend, and plans a large family. Pamina's mother, who has decided to try to effect a rescue herself, fails.*

STRANGE BUT TRUE
The flute was Mozart's least favourite instrument.

SHAMELESS PLAGIARISM
The Act II priests' march was "borrowed" from Wranitzky's *Oberon*, and the overture's main theme from a Clementi sonata.

WHAT THE PAPERS SAID
"Inferior." (*Musikalisches Wochenblatt*)

FELONY COUNT
Two attempted rapes, two attempted suicides, one abduction, incitement to murder, numerous instances of sexual discrimination and inciting racial hatred.

NOT TO BE CONFUSED WITH
Kaspar der Fagottist, a little number about a magic bassoon by Wenzel Müller, also produced in Vienna in 1791.

CRUSH BAR GAMBIT
"The *Flute* is nothing less than a *tour d'horizon* of religious history. The ancient matriarchal worship of the moon-goddess is overthrown by men. Pamina's acceptance symbolises the eventual assimilation of the idea of *Hagia Sophia* or holy wisdom by the misogynistic Graeco-Judaeo-Christian tradition. Clearly, Mozart would be in favour of women priests."

RECORDINGS
❖ Klemperer, Janowitz, Popp, Gedda, Berry, Philharmonia Chorus and Orchestra (EMI) ❖ Christie, Mannion, Kitchen, Blochwitz, Scharinger, Les Arts Florissants (Erato) ❖

Manon Lescaut

GIACOMO PUCCINI (1893)

Men couldn't resist her – but she loved only her jewels!

In short: *Manon's sugar-daddy arranges for her to be arrested as a prostitute. Her true love accompanies her into exile. They die.*

MUSIC

The third of Puccini's operas, and his first big hit; his technique develops as the opera progresses, trying out styles from Verdi to Wagner – with some 18th-century pastiche thrown in. His trademarks are already there: the pacing and drama of the music, rising to thunderous climaxes; the prodigal melodic invention; arias short enough to leave the audience wanting more; a rather thick hero and *demi-mondaine* heroine; heartbreak; death. The ensembles are better than the arias, and abound. Tenor's big tune: *No! pazzo son* (as he cadges a passage on the ship). Manon: *Sola, perduta, abbandonata* (as she pegs out in the desert). The finale of each of the first three acts outdoes the last in intensity. The embarkation of the prostitutes is a tremendous ensemble/chorus set piece. The last act, an extended *Liebestod*, can be genuinely affecting – Callas made it the highlight of the show.

WORDS

Cobbled together from the racy and one hopes only partly autobiographical writings of one Abbé Antoine-François Prévost, a twice-defrocked 18th-century priest. Many hands made an indigestible stew of the libretto before Puccini gave it to Giacosa and Illica, his collaborators thenceforth, to finish off. While far from atrocious by operatic standards, it cleverly manages to mystify by leaving out many crucial parts of the story.

PLOT

Act I *Amiens is full of roistering students as teen hotty Manon arrives, en route to the convent where, alas, she is to take the veil. A fellow-passenger in her coach, Geronte, a government minister, has taken a shine to her and, with the collusion of her brother, plans to abduct her. But the lovestruck Chevalier des*

Grieux, an impoverished aristocratic student, gets in first and whisks her off to a life of passion (and squalor) in Paris.

Act II Manon has got tired of household chores and is now installed in some splendour chez Geronte. But she misses her ardent student. Des Grieux shows up unexpectedly, they fall into a clinch, and are discovered by Geronte. He sends for the cops. A hurried exit is clearly the thing, but Manon can't decide which jewels to take for her escape with des Grieux, wastes time, and is arrested.

Act III Le Havre. Manon is embarked for deportation to Louisiana with a collection of prostitutes. Des Grieux begs the captain to take him on as a cabin-boy (without pay).

Act IV Manon and des Grieux trudge across the desert. They expire.

DON'T ASK
What on earth are Manon and Des Grieux doing in the desert in Act IV?

NOT TO BE CONFUSED WITH
Manon, by Jules Massenet, 1884. Same story *à la française*, with powder and minuets.

CRUSH BAR GAMBIT
"Manon is suffering from an acute case of thanatomania, convinced that everything except death is an illusion. This explains her obsessive inability to engage with reality, running away successively from home, convent, Geronte and Des Grieux (twice each) and finally whatever situation it is that precipitates her into the desert. It would be interesting to know more about her childhood."

RECORDINGS
❖ Sinopoli, Freni, Domingo, Covent Garden (DG) ❖ Levine, Freni, Pavarotti, New York Metropolitan (Decca) ❖

The Marriage of Figaro

WOLFGANG AMADEUS MOZART (1786)

A close shave for the barber and his beloved!

In short: *Various nuptial problems are resolved when Count Almaviva's wife dons her maid's outfit.*

MUSIC

The overture launches straight into the chaos of Beaumarchais's *folle journée* and the pace never slackens. Each act culminates in an ensemble finale complete with breathtaking coup, and the timing throughout is perfect. The characters of the original farce are transfigured by the music, and the way Mozart creates a universal moral from the final scene of forgiveness (a mere two lines in the libretto) is just a miracle. All the arias and ensembles are stunners, perhaps the most perfect being Cherubino's song *Voi che sapete*, the lovely *siciliano* letter duet, and Susanna's *Deh vieni, non tardar*.

WORDS

A sex comedy, like all the libretti written by Lorenzo da Ponte for Mozart. Da Ponte, a renegade priest of Jewish origins and father of several illegitimate children, had some experience to draw upon. A masterful reduction of Beaumarchais's play, the sequel to *The Barber of Seville*.

PLOT

Act I *The morning of Figaro and Susanna's wedding. She tells him their boss Count Almaviva is about to revive the practice of* droit de seigneur *specially for her. Figaro considers how to scupper this aim.*

Act II *Figaro sends an anonymous letter to the Count telling him the Countess will be meeting her lover in the garden at night; he also persuades Susanna to arrange a tryst with the Count at the same venue, but plans to send Cherubino* *(an amorous page whom the Count suspects of consorting with his wife) along in drag instead of Susanna.*

Act III *Susanna sets up the assignation, but Almaviva realises he's being taken for a ride; to get his own back he orders Figaro to marry the elderly Marcellina (to whom Figaro owes money). Fortunately Marcellina turns out to be Figaro's long-lost mother, so that wedding is cancelled and Figaro and Susanna's goes ahead.*

Act IV *Susanna and the Countess hide in the garden, having borrowed each other's clothes. The Count appears and serenades his wife, thinking she is Susanna. Figaro begins to make noisy advances to Susanna, and the Count (thinking it's his wife, of course) goes crazy. Eventually everyone is revealed as themselves and the Count, realising he's been comprehensively had, begs his wife's forgiveness. Everybody heads off to the pub.*

STRANGE BUT TRUE
William Beckford, creator of *Vathek* and Fonthill Abbey, paederast and serial liar, claimed that he wrote *Non più andrai*, the show's original smash hit (which became the Coldstream Guards' official slow march in 1787).

NOT MANY PEOPLE KNOW THAT
Count Almaviva was right all along about his wife: in Beaumarchais's sequel, *La mère coupable*, she gives birth to Cherubino's child.

CRUSH BAR GAMBIT
"Far from being 'the revolution in action' that Napoleon thought, *Figaro* is a reactionary allegory about the perils of liberalism. Almaviva abjures *jus primae noctis* and the world falls apart; da Ponte, a friend of Emperor Joseph II, was warning his patron of the dangers of his reforms."

RECORDINGS
❖ Östman, Bonney, Augér, Nafé, Hagegård, Salomaa, Drottningholm Court Opera Chorus and Orchestra (L'oiseau lyre) ❖ Giulini, Moffo, Schwarzkopf, Cossotto, Waechter, Taddei, Philharmonia Chorus and Orchestra (EMI) ❖

The Mastersingers

RICHARD WAGNER (1868)

It's a load of cobblers!

In short: *A man wins a song competition through trickery and cheating.*

MUSIC

The least ponderous of Wagner's later operas, this four-and-a-half-hour comedy is still hardly a laughing matter. An extraordinary masterpiece of construction and counterpoint, it contains some ravishing romantic music, culminating in Walther's Prize Song and visiting en route chorales, jovial folk-tunes, the rousing pomposity of the overture and – a Wagner rarity – an Act III quintet of serene beauty. Much of the drawn-out dialogue, too, is surprisingly tuneful, and most of Act II is a creation of unusual pace and geniality, leading to a finale of satisfactory ensemble uproar.

WORDS

With his usual magpie tendencies, Wagner gleaned the material from a variety of sources: the writings of the historical Hans Sachs, a story by E.T.A. Hoffmann, Goethe and so on. Hans Sachs is a surprisingly pleasant character – even if he turns out to be a Nazi in the end – and there is the bonus of the peculiar spectacle of a couple unrelated by blood embarking upon a seemingly normal inter-gender relationship.

PLOT

Act I Veit Pogner, Nuremberg plutocrat, has decided to marry off his daughter Eva, and has promised her to the winner of tomorrow's Midsummer's Day song contest. A travelling knight, Walther, who arrived yesterday, has fallen in love with Eva and decides to enter the contest. Sadly his attempts to join the local choral society – the Mastersingers (a prerequisite of competing) – end in disaster when he fails to obey the ridiculously large number of rules.

Act II Eva and Walther decide not to bother with the song contest and to elope instead, but are prevented by Hans Sachs, local cobbler and top mastersinger, who has however taken a shine to Walther. There follow some mistaken-identity

116

shenanigans with Walther's rival, the foolish town clerk Beckmesser, causing a riot by attempting to serenade Eva after the police-enforced curfew at 10pm.

Act III *Walther wakes up with a song on his lips, which he sings to Sachs, who transcribes the words. It is subsequently appropriated by Beckmesser, but when he sings it at the contest he seems to have trouble with Sachs's handwriting and fouls it up. Walther is then allowed to sing it properly and wins hands down.*

DON'T ASK

How come Walther's allowed to take part in the contest? Hasn't he already been disqualified? And where are all the other competitors?

RISING ABOVE IT

The première was conducted by Hans von Bülow, despite the fact that Wagner had run off with – and impregnated – his wife Cosima.

WHAT RUSKIN THOUGHT

"Of all the affected, sapless, soulless, beginningless, topless, bottomless, topsiterviest, tuneless, scrannelpipiest, tongs-and-boniest doggerel of sounds I ever endured the deadliness of, that eternity of nothing was the deadliest."

CRUSH BAR GAMBIT

"The unconscious self-revelation is astonishing. The Wagner-figure, Walther, may get his girl but in order to do so willingly colludes with the stultifying conformism of the rule-bound small-town pedants of the Mastersingers, a bunch of saloon-bar fascists whose innate racism and thinly-disguised violence would be laughable but for their long-term implications."

RECORDINGS

❖ Kubelik, Stewart, Kónya, Janowitz, Crass, Hemsley, Bavarian Radio Chorus and Symphony Orchestra (Calig) ❖ Sawallisch, Weikl, Heppner, Studer, Moll, Lorenz, van der Walt, Bavarian State Opera Chorus and Orchestra (EMI) ❖

Nabucco

GIUSEPPE VERDI (1842)

Losing their religion!

In short: *An eccentric Assyrian family – one is mad, one a crazed suicide, and two in love with the same man – embraces Judaism.*

MUSIC

Verdi's first big hit. Rossini said it must have been written by an artillery colonel, and it is certainly forthright stuff, featuring singalong choruses, onstage military bands, combative arias and ensembles, and bags of spectacle. Abigail's music is psychopathic coloratura, with huge, jagged leaps; the Lear-ish Nabucco rages and raves like a force of nature, and Zechariah is prophetically venerable. The love story takes a back seat – Verdi went so far as to lock his librettist in a room until he'd replaced a love duet for Fenena and Ishmael with a prophecy by Zechariah. Uneven but compelling, and containing Verdi's best-known tune, *Va pensiero*, a grand aria for the entire chorus.

WORDS

By Temistocle Solera, a Casanova-like figure who ran away with the circus as a lad. Later, it turned out that he had filched much of the libretto from an 1836 French play whose authors sued for royalties. Not terrible – bits have a simple grandeur – but, in parts, condensed to the point of total mystification.

PLOT

Part I 586 BC: *Jerusalem is being trashed by the Babylon team captained by Nebuchadnezzar (Nabucco), whose daughter Fenena the Israelis are holding hostage in the Temple. She is in love with Ishmael, former Israeli ambassador to Babylon, and is broadly pro-Israeli. Not so her highly-strung elder sister Abigail (also in love with Ishmael, and jealous as hell) who now bursts into the Temple with a platoon of Babylonian shock-troops, followed shortly by Papa himself. Zechariah, a prophet, is about to execute Fenena but Ishmael stops him, to general annoyance, and everyone is carted off to Babylon.*

Part II *Abigail finds her birth certificate, which shows she is illegitimate: so it looks like Fenena (who has become a Jew) will inherit the throne. Abigail decides to stage a coup while daddy is away. But he arrives just as she is doing so, and immediately proclaims himself a god. Bad idea: he is instantly struck down by a thunderbolt.*

Part III *Abigail takes advantage of Nabucco's indisposition (he is now a loony) by getting him to sign a death warrant for all the Israelis plus Fenena.*

Part IV *Nabucco stages a startling recovery and immediately converts from Baalism to Judaism when he sees Fenena being led off to execution. Suddenly terribly nice, he hurries off to stop the executions and let the Israelis go. Abigail, probably wondering what her family is coming to, does herself in.*

DON'T ASK
Is it normal for prophets to execute hostages, or is that more like a hobby?

WHAT THE CRITICS SAID
"Absolutely dreadful, and utterly degrading for Italy."
(Otto Nicolai, composer of *The Merry Wives of Windsor*)

BANG TO RIGHTS
The conductor of an 1847 production in Milan had his collar felt for "having directed in a manner obviously rebellious and hostile to the Imperial Government."

CRUSH BAR GAMBIT
"Verdi clearly had robust views on multiculturalism. The Israeli *gästarbeiter* in Babylon subvert the entire society with their fundamentalist, fanatical monotheism, which contrasts so sharply with the *laissez-faire* Baalist attitudes of the locals. The inevitable result is cultural degradation, moral collapse and social disintegration."

RECORDING
❖ Gardelli, Suliotis, Gobbi, Cava, Prevedi, Vienna State Opera
Chorus and Orchestra (Decca) ❖

Norma

VINCENZO BELLINI (1831)

Crazy about the Gaul!

In short: *A Roman consul with a taste for French virgins comes to a sticky end.*

MUSIC

Bellini is the least demonstrative and most loveable of the *bel canto* composers, with a melodic gift that looks back to Mozart and forwards to Chopin. His serene tunes – of which *Casta diva* is the perfect template – unfurl languidly over the simplest scoring (string arpeggios, plucked bass notes, the odd flute) and go on forever. *Norma* also comes with patriotic choruses – the rip-roaring *Guerra, guerra* – dramatic arioso and some Verdian moments of atmospheric orchestral music, particularly at the beginning of Act II. Best bits are the duet *Ah! Rimembranza!*, a classic, tender Bellini tune, Norma's tremendous Act II will-she-won't-she (kebab the kids, that is), and the final brilliantly-paced scene, ending as a real tear-jerker.

WORDS

A high-class, action-packed adaptation by Felice Romani of a play by Alexandre Soumet in which Norma actually does manage to kill her children. Not unindebted to *Medea* by Euripides.

PLOT

Act I *Some moon-worshipping Gauls are all fired up for a set-to with the Romans when head priestess Norma tells them to cool it. Her hidden agenda: she's in love with the local Roman commandant Pollione, indeed has gone so far as to have secretly had two of his children, in serious breach of her employment contract, which stipulates virginity. He, however, is now in love with another, to wit trainee moon-nun Adalgisa, and convinces her to run off to Rome with him. Adalgisa confesses all to Norma: a serious error. The three of them have a big row.*

Act II *Norma decides to kill her children and herself, but accomplishes neither. Adalgisa dumps Pollione, but only briefly. He is then arrested in the*

Gaulish temple (a capital offence). Norma confesses her shortcomings to everybody and hops onto the pyre with Pollione.

What the papers said
"Endeavouring to be sublime, he is too apt to become merely noisy."
(*The Examiner*)

Strange but true
The chorus *Guerra, guerra* was played, somewhat inappropriately, in Palermo Cathedral in 1848 to celebrate the (temporary) deposition of the Bourbons in Sicily.

Not many people know that
The première (at Milan) was wrecked by a faction organised by Giulia Samoiloff, mistress of the composer Pacini whose *Il Corsaro* was due to open a couple of days later.

Diet tips
Probably unwise to drink a Bellini (prosecco, peach juice) with your pasta alla Norma (aubergines, tomatoes, *ricotta salata*), a Catanian dish inspired by the opera and also perhaps by the fact that the first Norma was one Giuditta Pasta (who originally refused to sing *Casta diva*, finding it "repugnant").

Crush Bar gambit
"The peculiar fact that these ancient Gauls are worshippers of Irminsul, a tree-stump highly thought of by the Saxons and located in the Teutoburger Forest in Northern Germany, makes it plain that *Norma* is a satire on the French fondness for covering up a lack of indigenous culture with German imports, a habit that began with Meyerbeer and reached its apotheosis in the Franco-Prussian war."

Recordings
❖ Serafin, Callas, Stignani, Filippeschi; Serafin, Callas, Ludwig, Corelli. Both with La Scala Chorus and Orchestra, EMI ❖

Orphée aux Enfers

JACQUES OFFENBACH (1858, REVISED 1874)

A marriage unmade in heaven!

In short: A top god provides a tiresome violinist with grounds for divorce by ravishing his wife in the form of a bluebottle.

MUSIC

One of the most exhilarating scores in opera (or operetta, a form *Orphée* invented and perfected) composed, alarmingly, by one of music's great depressives. *Orphée* is like G&S without the respectability – and was immensely popular in Victorian London. The can-can is only one highlight in a prodigiously tuneful romp of bouncy rhythms, infectious choruses, patter songs, comical ballets, great silliness and equal intelligence. Showstoppers: Orpheus and Eurydice's Mozartian Act I quarrel; the gods' rebellion, including snatches of the (then subversive) *Marseillaise*; their rondo ridiculing Jupiter's double standards; Jupiter and Eurydice's duet, consisting of the letter *z* set to music straight out of Grand Opera (he's a fly, see).

WORDS

A witty subversion of classical mythology by Hector Crémieux, given a hand by Ludovic Halévy.

PLOT

Act I Orpheus and Eurydice's bourgeois mariage de convenance comes to an abrupt halt when she steps on a snake Orpheus has thoughtfully left in a cornfield in the hope of impeding her trysts with a shepherd. The shepherd, it turns out, is none other than Pluto, who carts her off to Hades. Orpheus arrives on

Mount Olympus, most unwillingly goaded by Public Opinion to reclaim his wife. PR-conscious Jupiter orders Pluto to return Eurydice to her husband and takes the other gods to Hades to make sure the handover takes place.

Act II In Hades Jupiter takes a fancy to Eurydice himself, and turns into a fly to accomplish her seduction. The other gods whoop it up and dance the galop with infernal rough trade. Orpheus and Public Opinion, unaccountably delayed, now appear. Jupiter says Orpheus can have Eurydice back on the admittedly meaningless condition that he doesn't look round on their journey back above ground, then detonates a thunderbolt to ensure he does just that. Eurydice remains in Hades as a bacchante, Orpheus returns to Arcadia, and everyone lives happily ever after.

NOT MANY PEOPLE KNOW THAT
The overture to the 1874 version was written not by Offenbach but by one Carl Binder.

WHAT THE PAPERS SAID
"This moral infection is a threat to our cultural existence."
(Gustave Chouquet)

MEMORABLE TRIBUTE
The punk *Can-can* of Bad Manners (1981). In contrast to Buster Bloodvessel, Offenbach never weighed over six stone.

CRUSH BAR GAMBIT
"Like all interpretations of Orphic myth, Offenbach's is a deeply serious parable about the hieratic role of the artist in society. Though a prisoner of vulgar taste, he is the only one who can raise the gods from their slumber and make them sing. Orpheus is a philosopher-priest, and as such, obviously, must remain unmarried."

RECORDINGS
❖ Plasson, Sénéchal, Mespré, Burles, Capitole de Toulouse Chorus and Orchestra (EMI) ❖ Edwards, Fieldsend, Hegarty, Patterson, D'Oyly Carte Opera (Sony: in English) ❖

Orpheus and Eurydice

CHRISTOPH WILLIBALD VON GLUCK
(1762)

Don't look now!

In short: *A man goes to great lengths to find his wife, then kills her.*

MUSIC

The death knell of *opera seria*: 90 minutes of concentrated emotion
conveyed by three singers and chorus without showy arias, a return to
drama served by music and an expression of the "noble simplicity" of
pure classicism. Gluck rewrote the thing for Paris (different voices, more
dancing, more instruments), and Berlioz made a composite version in 1869,
but the original has an unadorned symmetry and beauty lost in later versions.
Despite supernatural interventions it is all about human emotions, and
contains in *Che farò senza Euridice* one of opera's most heartbreaking
arias. Curiously, to our ears, the saddest music is written in major keys.
Showstoppers: the doleful opening chorus and Orpheus's *Chiamo il mio
ben così*, plangently echoed by a reedy chalumeau; the whole of Act II,
including the Dance of the Blessed Spirits and the amazing *Che puro ciel*,
a masterpiece of luminous orchestration and a rare attempt to depict
heaven in music.

WORDS

By Ranieri de' Calzabigi, a colourful character on the lam from a murder
rap in Naples, after Vergil, Ovid and any number of others. The credit for
ditching the interminable recit-aria formula of *opera seria* is perhaps largely
his, but opinions vary on his wilfully happy ending (in the original myth
Orpheus goes home alone and is torn to pieces by a bunch of neolithic
women's-libbers).

PLOT

Act I *Orpheus is making such a song and dance about his wife Eurydice's untimely death (she stepped on a snake, silly thing) that Cupid appears and offers him a free return trip to Hades to bring her back. There are two pointless conditions: a) Orpheus mustn't look at her, nor b) explain why. Orpheus, who isn't entirely stupid, realises this is going to cause trouble.*

Act II *Orpheus arrives at Hades and finds some unfriendly spirits and a schizophrenic dog barring his way. After he explains the situation to them their attitude softens somewhat and they let him pass. He reaches the Elysian Fields, finds Eurydice and leads her off.*

Act III *As foreseen, Eurydice is less than overjoyed by Orpheus's apparent nonchalance, and indeed goes so far as to say she wishes she'd remained in Hades. After much nagging she begins to hyperventilate (or is she faking?), and Orpheus turns round to administer first aid. She dies (again). Orpheus is on the point of killing himself when Cupid appears and says it was all just a bit of fun between the gods and actually he can have Eurydice back after all.*

MOST IMPROVED PRODUCTION
1792, Covent Garden: "Music by Gluck, Handel, Bach, Sacchini and Weisel with additional new Music by William Reeve."

WHAT HANDEL THOUGHT
"He knows no more of counterpoint than Waltz, my cook."

WHAT THE PAPERS SAID
"Its uneventfulness and monotony produce tedium." (*Mercure de France*)

CRUSH BAR GAMBIT
"The opera is hardly the portrayal of connubial love it is commonly thought: it is clearly a metaphor for the breakdown in communication familiar to many couples. Gluck's happy ending is deeply cynical: these two are obviously on the fast track to the divorce courts."

RECORDINGS
❖ Gardiner, Ragin, McNair, Monteverdi Choir, English Baroque Soloists (Philips: Vienna version) ❖ Gardiner, von Otter, Hendricks, Monteverdi Choir, Lyons Opera Orchestra (EMI: Berlioz version) ❖

Otello

GIUSEPPE VERDI (1887)

A tissue of lies!

In short: *Not many Venetian soldiers return from an overseas posting.*

MUSIC

Wheedled out of his post-*Aida* retirement by publisher Giulio Ricordi, Verdi emerged with a miraculous ability to capture the faintest nuance of character and drama in his music, and became the first composer to confront Shakespeare on something like level ground. Beginning with a crashing storm which puts the conventional niceties of weather-music firmly in their place, this is a score of immense sophistication, though done with the lightest of touches. The music describes how jealousy worms its way into Othello's brain, and turns Iago into something more than the libretto's panto villain, while Desdemona floats above it all on an unending line of serene melody. Showstoppers: Iago's jolly, sinister drinking song; the first love duet, as Desdemona's sweet melody melts the orchestra's thick tones; the Act II quartet, a tranquil tune above Othello's anguish and Iago's bullying; Iago and Cassio's locker-room scene, a piece of Mozartian elegance with quicksilver scoring; and Desdemona's last act, with the unearthly Willow Song.

WORDS

By Arrigo Boito, who ditched Shakespeare's first act and emerged with a libretto of great immediacy.

PLOT

Act I Othello, Venetian top brass, arrives in Cyprus with his new wife Desdemona. Iago, his ensign, has a grudge against him based on being passed over for promotion in favour of Cassio. He encourages Roderigo, a moron with a crush on Desdemona, to start a fight with Cassio, resulting in the latter's demotion.

Act II *Iago encourages Cassio to ingratiate himself with Desdemona, then makes sure that Othello notices and leaps to conclusions. He appropriates one of Desdemona's hankies, plants it in Cassio's house and offers to get Othello proof that his wife and Cassio are at it like bunnies.*

Act III *Othello has a row with Desdemona, asks where her hankie is and calls her rude names. Then he watches as Iago has a laddish chat with Cassio in which the latter reveals the hankie, which he assumes has been left as a come-on in his house by some slapper. At this inconvenient juncture some envoys arrive with instructions for Othello to return to Venice. During the summit he goes crazy and starts beating Desdemona up, to general surprise. He decides to kill her ...*

Act IV *... and does so a bit later. However the rest of Iago's plan has gone belly-up, all is revealed, he runs off and Othello stabs himself.*

FANCY THAT
In a change from the usual set-up, in a 1955 New Orleans production by the all-black Opera/South company Othello was the only white cast-member, called in at the last minute after the original singer and his understudy dropped out.

AUDIENCE REACTION
"I always said mixed marriages were a mistake, and that just proves it."
(Allegedly overheard at Covent Garden)

CRUSH BAR GAMBIT
"*Otello* is Verdi's admission that *bel canto* is dead and Wagner has won: Desdemona, the personification of his muse, must die for opera to survive; Verdi must throttle himself, and Iago, symbol of Wagnerian anti-music, whom Verdi, unlike Shakespeare, allows to escape, conquers."

RECORDINGS
❖ Chung, Domingo, Studer, Leiferkus, Bastille Opera Chorus and Orchestra (DG) ❖ Serafin, Vickers, Rysanek, Gobbi, Rome Opera Chorus and Orchestra (RCA) ❖

Parsifal

RICHARD WAGNER (1882)

No woman could corrupt him!

In short: *An itinerant fool performs first aid on an injured knight with his spear.*

MUSIC

Pervaded by massive sonorities of choral brass, string arpeggios and luxuriant orchestral textures, the best of *Parsifal* has a stately beauty, rising to vast, hair-raising climaxes. Wagner is a wizard of orchestration, and can change the scenery at a stroke with a slender oboe line. Sadly, he had also discovered that *andante* was the "specifically German tempo" (it's true!), but though *Parsifal* is the most ponderous and static of his works, it does have its lighter moments (inevitably associated with impurity) such as the ravishing flower-girl music. The leitmotivs are handily laid out in the prelude, so everyone knows what's what, and thereafter the music requires total submission: fighting against it only makes you uncomfortably aware of the four-hour-plus running time. Like it or not, most 20th-century music could not have been written without *Parsifal*.

WORDS

By Himself, of course. His last work is more religious rite than opera. The hero is Malory's Sir Percival, though Wagner took the story from Wolfram von Eschenbach's 12th-century version of events: legend is used as subject matter because of its putative universal relevance, a surprising prefiguration of Jung. Wagner uses a kind of dungeons-and-dragons language to convey the action, which is almost entirely interior. The implications of the libretto – an Aryanisation of Christianity – and the vaguely homoerotic society of militaristic black-clad blood brothers are, of course, deeply sinister.

PLOT

Act I Amfortas, head of a brotherhood of misogynous knights who have custody of the Holy Grail, is suffering from a wound he received from his spear during a reprehensible dalliance with comely Kundry, an employee of horrid wizard

Klingsor. The wound can only be healed by the touch of the same spear, but unfortunately Klingsor now has it and won't give it back. Parsifal appears and shoots a swan, to general disapproval.

Act II *Parsifal goes over to Klingsor's place, resists the blandishments of various shameless females, including Kundry, and gets the spear back.*

Act III *Several years later, Parsifal returns with the spear and cures Amfortas. This makes him flavour of the month, despite the delay.*

DON'T ASK
What kept you?

WHAT THE CRITICS SAID
"A disastrous and evil opera." (John Runciman)

STRANGE BUT TRUE
Wagner seemed to think that the name Parsifal, far from being plain old Percy, was Arabian and had something to do with the Parsees.

CRUSH BAR GAMBIT
"It is old hat to regard *Parsifal* as proto-Nazi; rather, it is purely a drama of sexual neurosis: Wagner's castration complex set to music. Both Amfortas and Klingsor are emasculated by women: one mentally, the other physically. If it were composed now, the opera would be called *Bobbitt*. Naturally, Kundry, the *Ewig-Weibliche*, must die at the end."

RECORDINGS
❖ Karajan, Hoffman, Vejzovic, Moll, van Dam, Nimsgern, Deutsche Oper, Berlin Philharmonic (DG) ❖ Barenboim, Jerusalem, van Dam, Holle, Meier, Berlin State Opera Chorus, Berlin Philharmonic (Teldec) ❖

The Pearl Fishers

GEORGES BIZET (1863)

Condemned to burn – for being in love!

In short: Leila, a singing lifeguard, allows romance to interfere with her duties, and gets the sack.

MUSIC

It has an unjustified reputation as a one-tune opera, although the tremendous tenor-baritone duet *Au fond du temple saint* is undoubtedly the top tune – as Bizet clearly knew, judging by the number of times it crops up. Unlike in *Carmen*, the exoticism sounds rather as though it fell off the back of a lorry: the odd chorus is uncannily like the witches in Verdi's *Macbeth*. But Bizet could not write a dull note, the shimmery orchestration is perfect and the somewhat languid air of the thing is set off against moments of high drama, particularly the Act II finale. Highlights include Nadir's gentle siciliano romance *Je crois entendre encore*; Leila and Nadir's love duet *Ton cœur n'a pas compris le mien* and their surprisingly jolly farewell to each other as they await the bonfire.

WORDS

Jobbing hacks Michel Carré and Eugène Cormon were commissioned to provide something exotic containing one or more vestal virgins, one priest of a religious cult, one pair of ill-fated lovers and one massacre (optional). They said later they would have tried a bit harder had they realised the quality of the music.

PLOT

Act I A Sinhalese community of pearl divers awaits the arrival of a woman they have hired to stand on a rock and sing (to keep the gods sweet) while they go about their business. Qualifications specify virginity; duties include remaining veiled and chaste. Zurga, the head diver, and his gloomily-named friend Nadir reminisce noisily about the time they nearly fell out over a woman from Kandy, but decided their friendship was more important and vowed never to see her again. Leila, the new rock singer, arrives. She is, of course, the woman from Kandy. She and Nadir recognise each other. It seems they had a bit of a thing together in spite of Nadir's vow. This also casts doubt on the accuracy of Leila's CV.

Act II Leila and Nadir tryst by night in breach of her employment contract, and are arrested. The fishermen want them killed but Zurga is for letting them go. Leila is unveiled, Zurga recognises her as the Kandy woman, is overcome with jealousy and decides they should die after all.

Act III Zurga struggles with his conscience, then procures Leila and Nadir's escape. This makes him unpopular with the locals, who kill him (or not, depending on which version is playing).

WHAT THE PAPERS SAID
"The libretto contains no fishermen, and the music no pearls." (*Le Figaro*)

NOT MANY PEOPLE KNOW THAT
The libretto was originally set in Mexico, not a place renowned for its pearl fisheries.

DON'T ASK
What *are* all those useless fakirs up to?

CRUSH BAR GAMBIT
"Given that those employed in Leila's capacity in Ceylon were invariably male, it is obvious that the opera is an elaborate pathico-troilist fantasy, and the eternal triangle at its centre distinctly scalene."

RECORDINGS
❖ Cluytens, Angelici, Legay, Dens, Opéra-Comique Chorus and Orchestra (EMI) ❖ Plasson, Hendricks, Aler, Quilico, Capitole de Toulouse Chorus and Orchestra (EMI) ❖

Pelléas et Mélisande

CLAUDE DEBUSSY (1902)

An innocent love – but still they had to die!

In short: A man kills his brother when he discovers him dallying with his educationally subnormal wife.

MUSIC

Pelléas is an opera without ancestors or descendants. Debussy freed himself from the bonds of diatonic harmony by the simple expedient of ignoring traditional rules of grammar and syntax: thus, while in themselves none of the chords he uses is shockingly innovative, the way he moves from one to another is. The music, in a very French way, is subordinate to the words, a gloss upon what is said and unsaid; this can result in rather a dearth of tunes, but the vast tone-poem of the orchestral score makes up for it. Debussy is much more sparing with brass instruments than Wagner and the result, despite a comparable orchestra, is a much lighter texture.

WORDS

The grandaddy of many atrocious French films. Maurice Maeterlinck is a justly forgotten Belgian playwright specialising in the inconsequential and the unexplained. The action takes place in a mythic, Wagnerian landscape of forests, towers, wells and other subconscious phenomena, largely unpopulated except by the dysfunctional and extended family of blind King Arkel. *Pelléas* is notable for a rare operatic appearance by a flock of symbolist sheep.

PLOT

Act I Golaud, lost in the forest, finds Mélisande, a tiresome girl with exceptionally long hair, weeping by a fountain. He marries her. After an unexplained absence of six months – perhaps an extended CenterParcs honeymoon – they return to the castle of King Arkel, Golaud's grandfather.

Act II Golaud's young half-brother, Pelléas, has a chat with Mélisande by a well, into which she stupidly drops her wedding ring. Golaud is very cross.

Act III *Mélisande sits by her window combing her hair. Pelléas comes by and ties her hair to a tree. Golaud appears and is cross again. Later, he spies on the pair of them, using his son Yniold as a periscope because his window is too high to see out of.*

Act IV *Golaud catches Pelléas and Mélisande in a clinch. He kills Pelléas.*

Act V *Mélisande has a baby and dies. There is a strong implication that Golaud will die shortly, too.*

Don't ask
Anyone fancy a pint?

Strange but true
Maeterlinck tried hard to wreck the première by writing rude letters to *Le Figaro* hoping for a "prompt and resounding flop". When he saw the opera he said: "For the first time I have entirely understood my own play."

Crush Bar gambit
"The big problem for the characters in *Pelléas* – as for all symbolists – is that they have become terrified to carry out even the simplest actions because, for example, the chair they are about to sit on might suddenly turn out to be not a chair at all but a symbol of sexual neurosis. This leads to an irrational horror of the material, and explains why Mélisande is so keen to get rid of all her possessions in the nearest water feature."

Recordings
❖ Abbado, Ewing, Le Roux, Van Dam, Vienna State Opera Chorus, Vienna Philharmonic (DG) ❖ Boulez, Söderström, Shirley, McIntyre, Covent Garden (Sony) ❖

Peter Grimes

BENJAMIN BRITTEN (1945)

Branded a child-killer – but still she loved him!

In short: *An antisocial fisherman is driven to suicide after a slump in his already debatable popularity following the deaths of his apprentices.*

MUSIC

Britten's first proper opera. His familiar shifting keys and cross-rhythms are distinctly brine-flavoured: the famous sea interludes continue beneath the action and flavour the whole score. The Borough gossips, a collection of buffoons and gawping yokels, bitch in jaunty recitative, work to the rhythms of sea-shanties and launch into thunderous choruses: the chilling refrain "Grimes is at his exercise" may stay with you for longer than you wish. In contrast, Peter's dreamy rendition of his "fiery visions" contrives to make him sympathetic and eventually tragic, despite his being a violent, schizophrenic misfit. Showstoppers: the scenes are truly indivisible, those that stand out being the pub scene (including Peter's visionary aria *Now the Great Bear and Pleiades*), Ellen talking to John as psalms drift out of the church, and Peter's desperate wanderings. The Act II women's quartet is an enchanting curiosity, like something out of Richard Strauss.

WORDS

By Montagu Slater after the 1810 Aldeburgh poem *The Borough* by George Crabbe, an effective study of the mechanics of mob rule. The theme of the persecuted outsider had obvious resonance for the homosexual conscientious objector Britten.

PLOT

Prelude *The coroner's court: Peter explains the death of his apprentice at sea. The verdict, delivered with snide insinuations, is accidental death; the towns-people are hostile, apart from Ellen, who fancies Peter.*

Act I *A storm brews. Peter tells the sympathetic Balstrode of his dreams to get rich and marry Ellen. He sends away for a new apprentice (bad move). Everyone takes shelter in the pub during the storm. The new apprentice, John, appears and Peter takes him home. The townspeople mutter their unspecified but sinister suspicions.*

Act II *Ellen talks to John outside church, and finds a bruise on his neck. She remonstrates with Peter; he socks her and storms off with John. The townspeople whip themselves into a rage and set off to confront Peter. Peter bullies the boy to get ready to go fishing. As they leave the hut John falls down the cliff, washed away by the storm, to his death (as it turns out). The townspeople arrive to find the hut empty, but surprisingly neat.*

Act III *A few days later; Peter and John have not reappeared. On the beach Ellen and Balstrode discover the boy's soaked jersey and Peter's boat. The townspeople get wind of it and a lynch-mob sets off. Ellen and Balstrode find Peter wandering derangedly in the fog. Balstrode tells him he'd better take his boat out to sea and sink it.*

DON'T ASK
How the good people of Aldeburgh took to their neighbour's depiction of them.

CRUSH BAR GAMBIT
"Of course, Peter's tragedy is irredeemably lower-middle-class: consider how bourgeois are his dreams of wife, money, respect, how pathetic the genteel tidiness of his hut! Grimes can only be seen as a tragedy of provincial *anomie* and the failure of imagination."

RECORDINGS
❖ Hickox, Langridge, Watson, Opie, London Symphony Chorus, City of London Sinfonia (Chandos) ❖ Britten, Pears, Watson, Pease, Covent Garden (Decca) ❖

Porgy and Bess

GEORGE GERSHWIN (1935)

Love ain't the drug!

In short: *A woman expresses a preference for the attractions of Bolivian Marching Powder and New York to life with a crippled beggar.*

MUSIC

Opera, operetta, musical – who really cares? Certainly operatic in conception, ambition and technical difficulty, *Porgy* is held together with melodic and rhythmic motifs and fuses jazz, Broadway and any number of other black and Jewish American musical forms into an unmistakeably individual style. *It ain't necessarily so, Bess, you is my woman now, Summertime* and *I got plenty o' nuthin'* may be the obvious showstoppers, but some of the very best bits are less well-known: the spirituals everyone bursts into at the drop of a hat, and the prayer scene and choruses Gershwin copied down when holidaying on a Gullah Negro island.

WORDS

From DuBose Heyward's novel *Porgy*; libretto by the author and Gershwin's brother Ira, who wrote the cleverer lyrics, eg, Sportin' Life's. Heyward was inspired to write the book by the adventures of one Goat Sammy, a member of the local low-life.

PLOT

Act I *A craps game in Catfish Row, a Charleston tenement populated by fisherfolk, is interrupted by the arrival of the singularly unpleasant Crown, a drunk, and his woman (not noted for long-term attachments) Bess. Crown immediately gets into character and kills someone, then legs it before the cops arrive. Bess shacks up pro tem with goat-powered cripple Porgy. The stupid, racist cops arrest a chap called Peter.*

Act II *Nearly everybody goes off to Kittiwah Island for a picnic (not Porgy: no disabled access). By coincidence, this is where Crown legged it to, and he detains Bess for private purposes. She turns up back at Porgy's two days later,* *in a state. Jake goes out fishing despite a gale warning in all areas. During the storm Crown turns up and has a fight with Porgy (no great contest). Then he runs out into the storm to help Jake's wife Clara, who has got into a tiz about Jake (now drowned). It is assumed they both die.*

Act III *Wrongly: that night Crown crawls up to Porgy's door. Porgy kills him. He is then required by racist and clearly stupid cops to ID the body but refuses to look at it, which gets him a week in the cooler. On his release he learns that Bess has upped and offed to New York with Sportin' Life, a smooth-talking coke dealer. He elects to follow in his goatcart.*

FANCY THAT

Gershwin financed the composition of *Porgy* by doing weekly radio shows sponsored by Feenamint, a laxative chewing-gum.

NAZI NOTES

They didn't like it: so much so that in Copenhagen in 1943 they said they would bomb the opera house if it wasn't taken off.

WHAT THE CRITICS SAID

"A highly unsavoury stirring-up together of Israel, Africa and the Gaelic isles … gefilte-fish orchestration." (Virgil Thompson)

CRUSH BAR GAMBIT

"It is a typically urban view of the decline of the provincial seaboard and its primitive fishing industry; to reinforce the point, even the loser Porgy is named after a fish – what we would call a bream. The Promised Land everyone goes on about is clearly *echt*-metropolitan Harlem."

RECORDINGS

❖ Rattle, White, Haymon, Blackwell, Clarey, Glyndebourne Festival Chorus, London Philharmonic Orchestra (EMI) ❖ DeMain, Albert, Dale, Lane, Shakesnider, Houston Grand Opera Chorus and Orchestra (RCA) ❖

I Puritani

VINCENZO BELLINI (1835)

Sects and love in Olde Englande!

In short: A cavalier's insistence on doing his patriotic duty drives his fiancée crazy.

MUSIC

Bellini in his usual tuneful form, but *Puritani* can seem a bit one-paced –
partly the fault of the libretto. One of his endearing features is an inability to
stay in a minor key for long, even in tragic circumstances. Among genuine
highlights, top comes Elvira's 15-minute Act II mad scene in which she runs
the gamut of lunacy with the help of some astonishing runs, trills and other
appurtenances of coloratura. There is some pleasant opening pageantry
(including an extremely High Church prayer scene, most unPuritan); the
jaunty *polacca, Son vergin vezzosa*, carefree aerobatics over a kind of patter
ensemble with a real Viennese swing to it; Elvira's initial bout of insanity, the
sweet *O vieni al tempo*; and Giorgio and Riccardo's otherwise totally
irrelevant duet *Suoni la tromba*, a welcome piece of upbeat soldierly bravado.
Earplugs ready for Arthur's truly frightening top F in the final ensemble.

WORDS

Even by the standards of *bel canto* this is a pretty threadbare libretto (Bellini
referred to its "stupid turns of phrase"), the responsibility of an Italian exile
in France, Count Carlo Pepoli, who took the story from a French play.

PLOT

*Act I The Puritan HQ in Plymouth, 1649, is gearing up for the wedding of
commandant Lord Walton's daughter Elvira to Cavalier Arthur Talbot, an earl.
This is a nice surprise for Elvira, who thought she was going to marry
Roundhead Sir Richard Forth: so did he, and he is pretty sore about it. But it
seems her kindly uncle George talked daddy round for her, and Arthur is given
a surprisingly warm welcome at the castle, given that he is an opponent in the
apparently still ongoing civil war. He then abuses their hospitality by running
off with a female prisoner suspected of being a Stuart spy (correctly: she is the*

recently widowed Queen Henrietta Maria). This seriously upsets Elvira, who goes mad.

Act II Richard magnanimously agrees with Uncle George that Arthur, now under sentence of death, will have to be pardoned and returned to Elvira to restore the balance of her mind. But first they have to find him.

Act III Handily, three months later he shows up unprompted. At this moment the civil war ends and he is pardoned by Cromwell. Elvira gets better.

BLUE PENCIL NOTES
In Rome it went by the title *Elvira Walton*, since Puritans, being Protestant, could not be mentioned (tricky, surely?).

WHAT THE PAPERS SAID
"Nothing can be more worthless than this opera; it is a mass of drivelling imbecility." (*The Spectator*)

ALSO KNOWN AS
I Puritani di Scozia, either because the librettist thought Plymouth was in Scotland (perhaps thinking of Lossiemouth), or maybe because he imagined he was adapting Scott's *Old Mortality* (in French *Les Puritains d'Écosse*), which he wasn't.

CRUSH BAR GAMBIT
"Elvira's 'madness' is a dramatic symbol of her lack of status as an unmarried women: her delirious loss of identity reinforces the point that with her chances of marriage up the spout she no longer exists as a politico-biological concept."

RECORDINGS
❖ Bonynge, Sutherland, Pavarotti, Ghiaurov, Luccardi, Caminada, Cappuccilli, Covent Garden (Decca) ❖ Serafin, Callas, di Stefano, Panerai, Rossi-Lemeni, La Scala (EMI: mono) ❖

The Queen of Spades

PYOTR ILICH TCHAIKOVSKY (1890)

Her heart was trumped – by a knave!

In short: *A romantic young woman dumps her fiancé for a suicidal monomaniac, then kills herself.*

MUSIC

As you would expect there are plenty of dances and songs and some really well worked-out scenes, notably the confrontation between Herman and the Countess; much of the ensemble music sounds like a ballet, rhythmically varied, always melodic, scored to perfection. There are lots of borrowings, above all from Mozart, and the drama lies largely in the contrast between this and Herman's increasingly overwrought music. The lengthy rococo pastorale in Act II is perfectly lovely but holds up the action a bit. The best arias are Herman's passionate Act I two-parter, *I do not know her name*, and Liza's wistful pre-suicide musings in Act III.

WORDS

Tchaikovsky and brother Modest made much more of a dog's dinner of Pushkin's pungent miniature than with *Eugene Onegin*: the setting is moved to 1790s Petersburg to accommodate the Mozart pastiche, Herman is transformed from Dostoyevskian prototype to romantic hero, and he and Liza are both killed off. The libretto was actually turned down by one Nikolai Klenovsky, a pupil of Tchaikovsky's.

PLOT

Act I Herman – a German – learns to his disappointment that the girl he loves, Liza, is engaged to another. He discovers that her granny, a decrepit Countess, once acquired the secret of winning at a rather stupid card game called faro (by sleeping with the satanic Count Saint-Germain) and feels this *information may be of some use. He pops up on Liza's balcony and is delighted to hear that she loves him right back.*

Act II *Following a party, Liza brazenly invites Herman to her bedroom. On the way he stops by the old lady's room and asks her to tell him her secret, but sadly she drops down dead when he pulls a revolver on her.*

Act III *The Countess's ghost pays a visit to Herman and tells him he needs to play the three, seven and ace. Liza, thinking Herman is more interested in cards than in her, takes an early bath in the nearest canal. Herman sets off to the casino, plays the cards to spectacular stakes and loses everything by idiotically playing the queen of spades instead of the ace. He shoots himself.*

STRANGE BUT TRUE

In 1888 Tchaikovsky wrote: "I am not going to write *The Queen of Spades* … it doesn't grab me and it would just turn out any old how."

NOT MANY PEOPLE KNOW THAT

The song the old lady sings as she remembers her Parisian youth (from Grétry's *Richard the Lionheart*) can only have been written when she was at least 75.

WHAT THE PAPERS SAID

"Interesting in parts." (*Novosti*)

CRUSH BAR GAMBIT

"Tchaikovsky's dance fixation, the result of his sexual terror, is a means of formalising and ultimately preventing inter-gender relationships. Like Puccini he equated sex and death; but Puccini at least allowed his characters to consummate their affairs before killing them off. For Tchaikovsky the emotion itself drives his characters to guilty madness and suicide."

RECORDINGS

❖ Gergiev, Grigorian, Gulegina, Arkhipova, Mariinsky Chorus and Orchestra (Philips) ❖ Ozawa, Atlantov, Freni, Forrester, Tanglewood Chorus, Boston Symphony Orchestra (RCA) ❖

Radamisto

George Frideric Handel (1720)

The family reunion from hell!

In short: *A dysfunctional extended family sorts out its differences.*

Music

Handel's first opera for the Royal Academy, generally performed in its much improved second version. Despite an unrelieved succession of recitatives and arias (31 of them), *Radamisto* holds the attention for its three-plus hours. Handel was the most feminist of composers, and this is an opera of wronged women, made theatrical by Handel's dramatisation of the emotions, from pride and rage to – mostly – grief and sorrow. A master of concision, he can suggest heartbreak in a well-placed pause like no other. Showstoppers include at least two of Handel's greatest arias: *Ombra cara*, a grief-stricken threnody backed by chromatic strings of heartbreaking intensity; and *Quando mai, spietata sorte*, a yearning cavatina with a Mozartian intertwining of soprano and oboe.

Words

A garbled version of an episode related by Tacitus concerning internecine war in the Caucasus in AD 51, modified by Nicola Haym from a play by Domenico Lalli that had already been set a couple of times.

Background

Now pay attention. Tiridate, King of Armenia, has invaded Thrace and taken its king, Farasmane, prisoner, all because he fancies Farasmane's daughter-in-law Zenobia. Tiridate's wife, Polissena, is Farasmane's daughter. One of Tiridate's generals, Tigrane, is in love with Polissena and is plotting a revolution. Radamisto, incidentally, is Farasmane's son, ie, Tiridate's brother-in-law, and is married to Zenobia. OK? (It could be worse: in the original Tiridate's brother Fraarte was also in love with Zenobia.)

PLOT

Act I *Tiridate besieges the Thracian capital. Radamisto and Zenobia decide to kill themselves.*

Act II *Radamisto and Zenobia wander disconsolately through the countryside, and she throws herself into the river Araxes rather than fall into Tiridate's hands. Happily, she is fished out alive downstream by Fraarte and taken to Tiridate. Radamisto is captured by Tigrane, who for reasons of his own takes him to Tiridate in disguise.*

Act III *Tiridate makes unsuccessful advances to Zenobia. Radamisto's cover is blown and Tiridate offers to spare his life if Zenobia will loosen up a bit. Luckily a revolution breaks out at this point; Tiridate apologises for his behaviour, promises to be nice to his wife from now on, and is forgiven by everyone.*

DON'T ASK
What became of Radamisto and Zenobia's Act I suicide pact?

GENDER CONFUSION
Considerable. Tiridate's generals, Fraarte and Tigrane, are sung by sopranos, though Fraarte was originally a castrato and Tigrane became one after starting life as a soprano. Radamisto is of course a counter-tenor (but was originally a soprano before becoming a castrato).

NOT MANY PEOPLE KNOW THAT
Handel postponed the première until King George and the Prince of Wales had made up their latest spat, in order to get both sets of hangers-on into the theatre. He blew most of the proceeds in the South Sea Bubble.

CRUSH BAR GAMBIT
"The correspondences between *Radamisto* and Hanoverian court life are obvious. Like Tiridates, George I had got sick of his wife (and locked her up for 32 years). Radamisto himself is clearly a cipher for the Prince of Wales, who, like many before and since, couldn't stand his father. Handel is treasonably suggesting the king was carrying on an affair with his daughter-in-law Caroline."

RECORDING
❖ McGegan, Popken, Gondek, Saffer, Dean, Freiburger Barockorchester (Harmonia Mundi) ❖

The Rake's Progress

IGOR STRAVINSKY (1951)

He diced with the devil – and drew!

In short: *A man's wishes come true: he goes mad and dies.*

MUSIC

Don't worry – this is Stravinsky in neo-classical mode, sounding in parts like an old LP of *Don Giovanni* left out for too long in the sun. The musical echoes extend from Monteverdi to Britten, though none of it could have been written by anyone but Stravinsky, whose longest score this is by some way. From the orchestra to the musical forms – aria, recit, arioso, ensemble – it sticks to 18th-century conventions and thereby emphasises how very 20th-century it is: smart, ironic, cynical. As with much pastiche the result can be rather cold-hearted until the final sad scene of Anne and Tom in Bedlam, but the score is full of humour and energy with some wonderful set-pieces. Showstoppers: the brothel scene, including the chorus of "whores and roaring boys", a paean to the sort of behaviour that would have Mr Blair marching them off to a cashpoint; the rumbustious auction scene; Anne's sweet lullaby, *Gently, little boat* and Tom's Didoesque death and threnody.

WORDS

Loosely based on Hogarth's paintings, which Stravinsky saw in Chicago in 1947. Advised by his Hollywood neighbour Aldous Huxley, he engaged his fellow American exile W.H. Auden to write the libretto, which he did with the help of his inconstant lover Chester Kallman. This is a high-quality if smart-arsed libretto which shares the score's mannered elegance.

PLOT

Act I *On the eve of his marriage to Anne Trulove, feckless Tom Rakewell fortuitously inherits a load of money and sets off to London with his saturnine new servant Nick Shadow, where he proceeds to blow the same in dodgy company.*

Act II *Nick persuades Tom to marry a bearded lady, Baba the Turk, for a laugh. This turns out badly, particularly when Anne appears on the doorstep after the wedding. Tom sinks his money in a machine he has dreamed up for turning stones into bread.*

Act III *This, perhaps not too surprisingly, is also less than successful and he goes bankrupt. Nick – who turns out to be none other than Old Nick – now demands payment, namely Tom's soul, as per his contract, but Tom finds a loophole in the small print. As a parting gesture Nick drives him mad, and he dies in Bedlam where Anne pays him a last visit.*

STRANGE BUT TRUE

A summer-of-love 1967 Boston production had the cast dressed up in Hawaiian shirts and watching TV.

HOW TO DEAL WITH CRITICISM

Confronted with some iffy reviews after a lacklustre première in Venice, Stravinsky merely waved his cheque, saying: "This is the only review I read."

CRUSH BAR GAMBIT

"Tom's journey is actually a gloomy determinist parable about the illusion of free will. His wishes for money, happiness and for his dreams to come true merely emphasise his enslavement to his own shadow, as does his self-consciously existentialist *acte gratuit* of marrying Baba. This latter-day Pilgrim's Progress is profoundly Calvinist: nothing you can do will alter your fate."

RECORDINGS

❖ Nagano, Hadley, Upshaw, Ramey, Bumbry, Lyons Opera Chorus and Orchestra (Erato) ❖ Ozawa, Rolfe Johnson, McNair, Plishka, Tokyo Opera Singers, Saito Kinen Orchestra (Philips) ❖

Rigoletto

Giuseppe Verdi (1851)

Joker gets the sack!

In short: *An aristocratic serial rapist demonstrates the advantages of wealth and charm.*

Music

A new departure: Verdi conceived *Rigoletto* in scenes rather than arias, and mixes tragic and comic opera routines, eg, by following the portentous prelude with the mocking dance-band that pervades the first scene. There is a new depth and development of character through music: viz the quartet *Bella figlia dell'amore*, a tremendous ensemble of mixed emotions. Other showstoppers are Gilda's delicate *Caro nome*, the engaging oompah chorus *Scorrendo uniti*, a spooky storm with pungent piccolos and chromatic humming chorus, and the inevitable *La donna è mobile*, which Verdi refused to give to the tenor until the dress rehearsal, fearing it would get out and overshadow the show.

Words

A faithful reduction by Francesco Maria Piave of Hugo's *Le roi s'amuse*, a play about naughty François I (the Field of the Cloth of Gold man), banned after its first performance in 1832. The Venetian censor was equally jumpy – kings just *don't behave* like that – the action was transferred to 16th-century Mantua and became a libel upon the Gonzaga family instead.

Plot

Act I *Rigoletto, an antisocial hunchbacked fool employed by the lecherous Duke of Mantua, teases Count Monterone, who is whingeing on about the Duke's seduction of his daughter. Monterone curses them both roundly. Rigoletto heads off home, where he is secretly keeping his daughter Gilda locked up for fear of the Duke's roving eye. Too late: the Duke has already sniffed her out, and Gilda is pretty keen on him, too. The Duke's pals, thinking she is Rig's secret mistress, decide to kidnap her for a laugh. Rigoletto, under the impression they're after the woman next door, idiotically gives them a hand.*

Act II *The Duke, happy to learn that Gilda is now locked up in his bedroom, slips off to rape her while his pals stall Rigoletto. Gilda emerges somewhat sadder but apparently no wiser. Rigoletto enters negotiations with a hit-man, Sparafucile.*

Act III *Sparafucile lures the Duke to his pub using his sister Maddalena as bait. Rigoletto fails to cure Gilda of her love for the Duke by making her watch him and Maddalena together. He tells her to clear out of town, in drag. Maddalena persuades her brother not to kill the Duke. Needing a body, Sparafucile kills the next passer-by: this happens to be Gilda, who has decided to sacrifice herself. Rigoletto takes delivery of the body in a sack and has a quick gloat. Then he hears the Duke singing in the pub. He undoes the sack and finds Gilda, still alive, but not for long.*

DON'T ASK

This curse only seems to work on Rigoletto. Is the Duke immune in some way?

WHAT THE PAPERS SAID

"No chance of staying in the repertoire." (*Gazette Musicale de Paris*)

CRUSH BAR GAMBIT

"*Rigoletto* is Verdi's atheistic version of *Don Giovanni*, Mozart's vengeful God reduced to an amalgam of a bungling cripple with a serious case of double standards and a businesslike hitman for whom any body will do. The message is, if you gotta do it, better do it yourself."

RECORDINGS

❖ Serafin, Callas, di Stefano, Gobbi, La Scala (EMI) ❖ Bonynge, Sutherland, Pavarotti, Milnes, Ambrosian Opera Chorus, London Symphony Orchestra (Decca) ❖

Rinaldo

GEORGE FRIDERIC HANDEL (1711)

Soul survivors!

In short: *Crusaders slot two easy conversions against Saracens.*

MUSIC

The cool, dotted rhythms of the overture announce the arrival of the 18th century and of Handel in England, and this joyous score has the clarity of the Enlightenment translated into music. Nearly three-quarters of the music is recycled, and Handel's famed two-week composition actually amounted to little more than transposition, new word-setting, and the composing of new recits, which are of unexpectedly high standard. The highlight for most people will be the languid saraband *Lascia ch'io pianga*, but there are many others: the piping recorders of Almirena's *Augeletti*, Rinaldo's Purcellian *Cara sposa* with its tortured chromatic strings, lots of rousing drum-and-trumpet music, and a splendidly varied role for the minxy Armida.

WORDS

Impresario Aaron Hill's libretto, translated into Italian by Giacomo Rossi, was designed to make fullest use of his flair for flying machines, dragons, magic transformations and other theatrical wonders (which included having some real birdies flying around during *Augeletti*, with unfortunate results for the audience's heads). Hill was sacked after the second performance.
The main source of the story is Tasso's *Gerusalemme Liberata*.

PLOT

Act I *Godfrey de Bouillon (Goffredo) and his crusaders are beating up the Saracens in Jerusalem. His right-hand man Rinaldo reminds Godfrey that he's been promised Godfrey's sister Almirena after the show's over. Godfrey stupidly grants the Saracen boss Argante's request for a breather, during which Argante enlists the help of his girlfriend the sorceress Armida, who kidnaps Almirena. Rinaldo decides to go and look for her.*

Act II *On Armida's magic island Almirena is fending off the advances of Argante. Rinaldo arrives, Armida takes a fancy to him and turns herself into Almirena, a trick which the dope Rinaldo keeps falling for. Argante also makes the mistake of having a crack at Armida while she's being Almirena, with unfortunate consequences for their relationship.*

Act III *Godfrey and his army now arrive to rescue Rinaldo and Almirena, taking notes from a hermit who, bizarrely, rents a cave on Armida's island. Most of the army is eaten by monsters but finally Godfrey and his remaining lads de-magic the place, release the captives and turn their attention back to besieging Jerusalem. They win the subsequent battle, Armida and Argante (now back together) decide Christian magic is better than theirs and join the Church of England.*

WHAT THE PAPERS SAID
"Filled with Thunder and Lightning, Illuminations and Fire-works; which the Audience may look upon without catching cold, and indeed without much danger of being Burnt; for there are several Engines filled with water, and ready to play at a minute's warning." (*The Spectator*)

CRUSH BAR GAMBIT
"Handel's subversive comment on the Act of Settlement and Hanoverian succession, *Rinaldo* suggests, with its shape-shifting heroine, that there is not much difference between the Protestant bigot Queen Anne, the Catholic bigot James the Old Pretender, or indeed Handel's old boss George of Hanover, and the superficiality of Armida's conversion merely reinforces the point."

RECORDING
❖ Malgoire, Watkinson, Cotrubas, Esswood, Scovotti, Grande Ecurie (Sony) ❖

The Ring of the Nibelung

RICHARD WAGNER (1876)

A rambling tale of a large-scale power struggle involving gods, giants, dwarves and the occasional human (but no editors).

WORDS

Twilight of the Gods was the first of the *Ring* librettos to be written (in 1848, under the name *Siegfried's Death*); only after writing the words did Wagner realise he'd have to fill in a bit of background, eventually amounting to *The Rhinegold*, *The Valkyrie* and *Siegfried*. His main sources were the Icelandic Eddas and *Volsunga Saga* and the German *Nibelungenlied*, itself a version of the Edda.

MUSIC

Whatever your resistance to Wagner – and every free-born Briton comes equipped with a varying amount – it is practically impossible not to be overwhelmed by the sheer power of the *Ring*. *Rhinegold* begins with a serene 136-bar meditation on the chord of E flat major, out of which all the subsequent themes emerge. The final scene contains some of Wagner's most ravishing music, six harps performing arabesques around airy strings and noble brass. The transformations between the scenes are his greatest tone-paintings, the hellish mines of Nibelheim allowing him to go crazy with 18 anvils, among other things, and there are some lovely tunes, notably from the Rhinemaidens and Froh, one of your less gloomy gods.

The Valkyrie is the high point of his leitmotiv system, a stunning synthesis of words and music, motifs passed seamlessly around the orchestra, combined and overlaid into an amazingly sophisticated commentary on the action. It is the most approachable work, with Straussian love music, heart-wrenching tenderness as Wotan says goodbye to Brünnhilde, an ecstatic playout as fire engulfs the mountain, and Wagner's loudest music, the Ride of the Valkyries. Act II is the heart of the whole drama, as the loopholes in Wotan's plans become apparent.

Wagner produces some of the darkest music ever written in *Siegfried*, with the help of double-bass tubas and a vast orchestra, but can also conjure the most delicate ethereality. The end of each act produces a marathon blaze of optimism, raw power (Act I), anticipation (II) and all-consuming ecstasy (III). *Forest Murmurs* bring a spot of pastoral relief.

Twilight of the Gods, the suitably earth-shattering climax, is the most "operatic" of the entire cycle, and Wagner's hugest architectural achievement. High spots include the Rhine cruise, the Rhinemaidens' return (one of the few bits of purely vocal magic in the cycle), some chilling but effective (and very loud) music from horrible Hagen and his hangers-on in Act II, Siegfried's overwhelming death march, and the final 20 minutes: Brünnhilde's increasingly radiant paean to Siegfried and the ecstatic playout, as the general mayhem eventually subsides into a theme of transcendent peace.

The Rhinegold (1854)

Finders keepers – but not for long!

In short: *A hot item of jewellery changes hands several times.*

Plot

Scene I *Alberich, a fascistic dwarf or Nibelung, appropriates some gold from some subaqua lovelies in the Rhine and forges a ring which he is reliably informed will make him Führer. (It also works as a mobile phone.)*

Scene II *On a nearby mountain Wotan, a god, is thinking about how not to pay the bill for the construction of his new castle, Valhalla. The builders take his sister-in-law hostage, which is a pity because she is the only green-fingered god and without her tending the kitchen garden there is nothing for anyone to eat.*

Scene III *Under pressure from his wife and peckish in-laws, Wotan sets off with his pyromaniac property-surveyor-cum-foreign-policy-adviser, Loge, for the Nibelung mines to kidnap Alberich and get his hands on the gold.*

Scene IV *Alberich ransoms himself with the gold and places a curse on the ring which will have severe long-term consequences for all involved. Wotan hands it all over to the builders, one of whom then beats the other to death (= curse already working). The sale of Valhalla is thereby completed and the god family moves in.*

If this ring is supposed to be all-powerful, how come it's so easy to relieve people of it?

Wagner claimed the music came to him while he lay in a trance in La Spezia in 1853.

"*Rhinegold* is a legal minefield. Has the gold in the Rhine been reduced into possession? If so, Wotan holds it on trust for the Rhinemaidens; if not, it surely belongs to Alberich, as does Valhalla, under the principle *nemo dat quod non habet*. Wotan is probably guilty not only of theft, conspiracy, extortion and being an accessory to murder, but is also liable for conversion and breach of trust. Of course, as a god it is possible he could claim benefit of clergy."

The Valkyrie (1856)

Fired!

In short: *A magic sword unexpectedly fails to work, and a Valkyrie takes a long kip.*

Plot
The gold which changed hands so often in Rhinegold *is now the property of a dragon, Fafner, latterly a giant. Wotan badly wants it back, and has fathered a pair of semi-human twins in the hope that they will do his dirty work, plus nine entirely divine Valkyries, a crack squad of female airborne paramedics. He has also left a magic sword lying around for anyone who might need it.*

Act I *Sieglinde is just buffing her husband Hunding's helmet when a hairy stranger bursts in. They immediately hit it off, but things end badly when Hunding comes home and it turns out that their guest was responsible for massacring his relations not long ago. Hunding arranges to kill his guest after breakfast (strict rules of hospitality prevailing). It turns out that the guest is Sieglinde's long-lost twin brother; they celebrate their reunion (while Hunding takes a kip) by having sex, giving him a name (Siegmund) and then doing a runner, taking the sword they find sticking out of the tree which is the main feature of Sieglinde's front room.*

Act II Wotan is getting it in the neck from his wife for allowing Sieglinde and Siegmund to have it off, and for planning to help Siegmund (via magic sword) in his forthcoming duel with Hunding. Brünnhilde, head Valkyrie, decides to give Siegmund a hand anyway, but Wotan marmelises the sword and Siegmund is killed. Brünnhilde rescues the now pregnant Sieglinde and packs her off to a forest to give birth to Siegfried.

Act III Wotan gives Brünnhilde the sack for insubordination and knocks her out on a mountain-top where she will become the property of the first rambler to penetrate the flames he thoughtfully surrounds her with.

WHAT THE PAPERS SAID
"So revolting, indecent and impure that it ought never to have been tolerated on the English stage." (*The Era*)

HANDY HINT ON SINGING BRÜNNHILDE
"Always wear sensible shoes." (Kirsten Flagstad)

HANSLICK'S VIEW
"This tuneless, plodding narrative recalls the mediaeval torture of waking a sleep-crazed prisoner by stabbing him with a needle at every nod."

CRUSH BAR GAMBIT
"*Valkyrie* is an anti-intellectual, anti-feminist diatribe concerning the dangers of abjuring the patriarchal system. All Wotan's carefully laid plans go pear-shaped when he allows himself to be browbeaten first by his wife and then his daughter, who are both cleverer than him. His problem is that he is both stupid *and* unsubtle."

Siegfried (1869)

The family that sleeps together keeps together!

In short: A bold but academically challenged German undresses an unconscious Valkyrie, and finds it a whole lot scarier than killing a singing dragon.

PLOT
Act I Siegfried, orphaned product of an incestuous one-night stand (Sieglinde died giving birth to him), has been thoughtfully adopted by Mime, Alberich's

little brother. They do not get on. Siegfried makes a sword.

Act II With this sword he proceeds to kill the dragon Fafner (who used to be one of the builders Wotan quarrelled with) and pockets the ring. Then he kills Mime for good measure. A talking bird, operating as a dating agency, arranges a meeting with Brünnhilde.

Act III Guided by the bird, Siegfried arrives at Brünnhilde's mountain. He shouts at her until she wakes up, whereupon they fall in love.

SOUNDS FAMILIAR

The dragon for the first production was made in England. Its neck never arrived (it finally turned up in Beirut).

CRUSH BAR GAMBIT

"*Siegfried* is a classic case-history of the regrettable genetic results of inbreeding. Its hero clearly believes that sociopathy starts at home: not content with tormenting the local wildlife, he murders his long-term guardian, beats up his grandfather and has sex with his aunt, while under the impression that she is his mother."

Twilight of the Gods (1874)

Everybody gotta go!

In short: *The return of a ring to its rightful owners somehow necessitates a large number of deaths.*

PLOT

Alberich, following Wotan's example, has fathered the revolting Hagen (by a certain Mrs Gibich, for a fee) in the hope that he will be able to get the ring back. Now Hagen plans to use his half-siblings Gunther and Gutrune to accomplish the task …

Act I *Siegfried and Brünnhilde emerge from their cave after an apparently successful first date. After giving Brünnhilde the ring Siegfried heads off down the Rhine for a spot of massacring, but is waylaid by the Gibichs. The sun is over the yardarm, and Gutrune gives Siegfried a cocktail which wipes out his memory; in very short order he gets engaged to Gutrune, promises to obtain Brünnhilde for Gunther and sets off to fetch her. She is understandably flustered when Siegfried turns up disguised as Gunther. He takes the ring back off her and they spend another night together, this time allegedly without any hanky-panky, though this will become a bone of contention later on.*

Act II *A double wedding is arranged but things do not go smoothly as Brünnhilde raises doubts about the exact events of the previous night.*

Act III *During a hunting party Siegfried is waylaid by the Rhinemaidens, who ask if they can have their ring back. He says no. Shortly afterwards he is murdered by Hagen. Brünnhilde finally understands what's going on, commits suttee on Siegfried's funeral pyre and gives Loge the go-ahead to torch Valhalla and its inhabitants. The Rhinemaidens finally get their ring; everybody else (except Alberich) dies, either by drowning or combustion.*

WHAT TCHAIKOVSKY THOUGHT
"With the last chords, I felt as though I had been released from prison ..."

CRUSH BAR GAMBIT
"The events at the Burgundian court of the Gibichs obviously represent the treacherous behaviour of Napoleon III in the run-up to the Franco-Prussian War. Brünnhilde is equally clearly a cipher for Bismarck, whose skilful editing of the Ems telegram provided the final impetus."

FURTHER READING
Why not have a crack at *Penetrating Wagner's Ring* (Associated University Presses, 1978), uphill going at first but full of meaty stuff.

RECORDINGS
❖ Barenboim, Jerusalem, Tomlinson, Evans, Kang, Bayreuth Festival Chorus and Orchestra (Teldec) ❖ Solti, Windgassen, Hotter, Flagstad, Nilsson, Frick, Vienna Philharmonic (Decca) ❖

Rodelinda

GEORGE FRIDERIC HANDEL (1725)

Upstart with a heart!

In short: *A north Italian kingdom keeps changing hands with remarkably little loss of life.*

WORDS

Slightly surprisingly based on fact gleaned from the 8th-century *Gesta Langobardorum*. Corneille's 1652 play *Pertharite* was turned into a libretto by Antonio Salvi which was then thoroughly plagiarised by Handel's librettist Nicola Haym. One of his most theatrically satisfying texts, concentrating as it does on the characters rather than tiresome political intrigues.

MUSIC

Amazingly, Handel's third big hit in a year, following *Julius Caesar* and *Tamerlano*, all composed for the Royal Academy, and for its succession of gorgeous arias perhaps the best of the lot. It contains some of his subtlest and best-characterised music for the self-indulgent sensualist Grimoaldo (a rare early starring role for a tenor), indecisive Bertarido and unhappy but spirited Rodelinda. The music progresses from poignant grief at the beginning to a tempered Enlightenment ideal of happiness reinforced by suffering. Of course it all sounds effortless, a facility Handel shared with Mozart, but is full of the art that conceals art, as in for example the magical and barely perceptible transition from recit to aria in Bertarido's *Dove sei*. Highlights: *Dove sei* and *Ombre piante*, a pair of sad arias mirroring each other, the first full of drooping cadences, the other with the soprano line echoed and pointed with solo recorder and violin; Rodelinda and Bertarido's heartbreaking separation duet *Io t'abbraccio*; *Chi di voi*, perhaps Handel's greatest prison scene.

PLOT

Act I Bertarido, King of Lombardy, has been foully usurped by Grimoaldo and has apparently died in exile. Grim makes unsuccessful overtures to Bert's wife Rodelinda, for which he is roundly abused by Eduige, Bert's sister, who reminds him they're engaged. Bert, who is not dead at all but is hanging around dressed as a Hun, is disappointed to overhear Linda eventually agree to marry Grim following threats from the latter's henchman Garibaldo.

Act II However, Linda's consent has a caveat: Grim must kill her son Flavio, which she knows he is too much of a softie to do. Bert now reveals himself to Linda and is promptly arrested by Grim.

Act III Bert escapes from prison and kills Gary. Grim, perhaps realising that things are rather stacking up against him, professes friendship for all and claims it has all been a terrible mistake. Everyone reverts to status quo ante.

DON'T ASK
Wouldn't a Hun rather stand out in Milan?

NOT MANY PEOPLE KNOW THAT
Rodelinda was first sung by Francesca Cuzzoni, the original prima donna, famous not only for scratching her rivals' eyes out on stage but also for poisoning her husband.

CRUSH BAR GAMBIT
"*Rodelinda* is the ultimate Machiavelli musical. Grimoaldo's downfall is a result of his failure of will: if he wants Rodelinda and the throne he should be prepared to act with a little fortitude and kill both Bertarido and Flavio. As it is he fails to play the fratricidal Bertarido at his own game and ends up with the ghastly Eduige. No doubt Bertarido, having learned a thing or two from the Huns, will lose no time in having Grimoaldo done away with and resuming his tyrannical rule."

RECORDINGS
❖ Schneider, Schlick, Schubert, Prégardien, La Stagione (Harmonia Mundi) ❖ Kraemer, Daneman, Taylor, Thompson, Raglan Baroque Players (Virgin) ❖

Der Rosenkavalier

RICHARD STRAUSS (1911)

She gave up her lover – for love!

In short: A boorish baron loses his fiancée to a teenage transvestite.

MUSIC

A conscious departure from the expressionist *Elektra, Rosenkavalier* is lavishly romantic and sentimental *à la* Viennese: more *schlag* than schmaltz, as befits a Strauss (even though the composer was unrelated to his waltzing namesakes). Strauss's most characteristic music has swooping violins and women's voices moving in parallel thirds or sixths, and his three sopranos give him plenty of opportunity to indulge. The waltz-soaked score gives way to bittersweet, contemplative arias, love duets of great delicacy and rumbustious ensembles, and the Marschallin's eventual renunciation of Octavian is truly affecting. Strauss has a light touch with his vast orchestra (and with his post-Wagnerian system of leitmotivs) and the final trio is 20 minutes of rarefied delight preceded by a breath-holding moment of stasis learnt from Mozart and Rossini.

WORDS

A largely successful attempt by Viennese poet and playwright Hugo von Hoffmansthal to produce a hybrid of the romantic comedy of *The Marriage of Figaro* and the knockabout farce of *Falstaff*, set in Maria Theresa's mid-18th century Vienna. Some of the humour is rather broad, notably the character of Baron Ochs.

PLOT

Act I The Marschallin (32) is indulging in a spot of extra-marital malarkey with 17-year-old Count Octavian (a mezzo in drag) when her rustic cousin Baron Ochs barges in. Octavian hurriedly dons chambermaid's gear and pretends to be the Marschallin's new maid; a mistake, as Ochs then attempts to have sex with him. Ochs needs a go-between to present a silver rose to his intended, Sophie (15). The Marschallin proposes the supposedly absent Octavian for the job.

Act II *Octavian presents the rose to Sophie and, not amazingly, they immediately fall in love. Ochs appears; Sophie's father is delighted that his daughter is marrying quality but Sophie is horrified by her first sight of her betrothed. Octavian is keen to prevent the wedding, and there is a scene.*

Act III *Ochs is set up: Octavian (in his chambermaid outfit) arranges a tryst with him at a local pub and has them discovered by Sophie's father, among others. Ochs narrowly escapes arrest for child abuse. The Marschallin realises it's time to get herself a new toyboy.*

DON'T ASK
What on earth is the Marschallin doing in the pub?

WHAT STRAVINSKY THOUGHT
"Cheap and poor."

STRANGE BUT TRUE
Elisabeth Schwarzkopf once had to hurriedly sew a pocket into her dress at the Met to dispose of an offering left in her lap by a puppy during the levée scene.

CRUSH BAR GAMBIT
"The gender confusion of *Rosenkavalier* is a clue that the Marschallin – whose name, not coincidentally, is Maria Theresa – is to be taken as a cipher for Kaiser Bill, who like his Hapsburg alter ego was soon to become *ancien régime*. The Bavarian Strauss was having fun at the expense of the Prussian monarch who had called the composer 'that viper I have nursed in my bosom', and who by the way had also banned the waltz."

RECORDINGS
❖ Kleiber, Reining, Jurinac, Gueden, Weber, Vienna Philharmonic (Decca) ❖ Karajan, Stich-Randall, Schwarzkopf, Ludwig, Edelmann, Philharmonia Orchestra (EMI) ❖

Salome

RICHARD STRAUSS (1905)

Wanted – dead or alive!

In short: *A Middle-Eastern potentate finds his lap-dancing bill is somewhat larger than expected.*

MUSIC

Times change, and these days you are more likely to drown in the relentless sensuousness of this score than die of moral outrage. This is the last word in romanticism, a swooning, chromatic river of music lasting a hundred uninterrupted minutes. Salome, "a 16-year-old with the voice of Isolde", reaches an immense climax, beautiful and faintly repulsive, as she serenades John's head to the wholehearted accompaniment of the 105-strong orchestra. John sounds like a man singing hymns in the bath. The title role, as ever, is a marvellous demonstration of the possibilities of the soprano voice. The famous dance is a piece of harmless would-be exotica: *Lawrence of Arabia* meets Johann Strauss.

WORDS

Oscar Wilde's etiolated 1891 play, written for Sarah Bernhardt but never performed by her, was for some reason a huge hit in Germany in its translation by the anarchist Hedwig Lachmann. Strauss abridged the text himself, probably relishing the infamy he knew it would bring. The inconsequential chatter owes something to Maeterlinck (cf *Pelléas et Mélisande*).

PLOT

It is Herod's birthday party. He keeps giving his step-daughter (also niece) Salome disgusting looks so she wanders onto the terrace and expresses an interest in the noises coming from a cistern. It seems that one Iokanaan – John the Baptist – is down there; he is carrying on in no uncertain terms about Salome's mother, Herodias. Salome says she'd like to meet him, and persuades Herod's top bodyguard, Narraboth, who is in love with her, to bring the man out. Salome likes the look of him – she is particularly keen on his mouth.

John tells her she's a horrible little girl and goes back to his well, not before
Narraboth has inexplicably and stupidly killed himself. Herod asks Salome to
dance for him, payment to be discussed later. She does her strip-tease and asks
for John's head. How about jewels, peacocks, a new sports chariot? says Herod.
No thanks, says Sal. Eventually he gives in. She gets the head, and talks dirty
to it. This is all too much for Herod. Kill her, he says. His heavies mash her
with their shields.

DON'T ASK
Hang on, wasn't it all her mum's idea?

FANCY THAT
The Austrian première, at Graz in 1906, was attended by Schönberg,
Webern, Berg, Zemlinsky, the Mahlers, Puccini ... and Adolf Hitler,
who had to beg the price of a ticket.

WHAT THE CRITICS SAID
"Perverted – like having countless beetles crawling around inside your
breeches." (Richard's father Franz Strauss)

CENSORSHIP NOTES
An unlikely alliance of the Lord Chamberlain, Kaiser Bill,
Archbishop Piffl of Vienna and J. Pierpont Morgan kept it off
the stage in a number of countries.

CRUSH BAR GAMBIT
"Like all the Germans, Strauss rather missed the point of Wilde's play,
a rather amusing satire on the Aesthetic movement and its attenuated
fin-de-siècle sensibilities. Herod's only objection to beheading John is on
grounds of *taste*: the head of a man separated from its body is an ugly thing,
as he says. Salome is a martyr to artistic progress, Herod a mad William
Morris-type idealist, John a gynophobe Ruskin."

RECORDINGS
❖ Solti, Nilsson, Waechter, Stolze, Hoffman, Vienna Philharmonic
(Decca) ❖ Sinopoli, Studer, Terfel, Hiestermann, Rysanek, Berlin
German Opera Orchestra (DG) ❖

Samson and Delilah

CAMILLE SAINT-SAËNS (1877)

Bringing the house down!

In short: *Gaza suicide attack destroys temple: many dead.*

MUSIC

Muscular, fugal choruses and stately action give *Samson* the flavour of an
oratorio, which is how it started life; but in its spectacle, dances and extended
Act II love duet it is a genuine blend of French grand and lyric opera.
Saint-Saëns was one of the most fluent of musical prodigies, but it took him
10 years to write Samson, some of it in London where he was taking refuge
from the Franco-Prussian War and Commune. Very French in its elegance
and clarity, it is heavily influenced by Bach, Handel and Mendelssohn, and
the love duet, culminating in the falling chromatics of Delilah's fantastically
languid and seductive *Mon cœur s'ouvre a ta voix*, is one of the most ravishing
in opera. The well-known bacchanal and dances provide by-the-yard
(and very attractive) oriental exoticism, a sort of French *Scheherezade*.

WORDS

A version by Fernand Lemaire of the unwanted-haircut episode from the
Book of Judges.

PLOT

Act I *Samson tries to cheer up the Jews, languishing in Palestinian captivity,
and whips them into such a frenzy they begin to riot. The Palestinians,
knowing Samson has something of a soft spot for the ladies, send out Delilah,
their secret weapon. Samson is thoroughly taken in, despite realising that
Delilah is probably a Bad Thing.*

Act II *Delilah waits for Samson in her country retreat, planning revenge:
it seems they had a one-night stand but he is now off frolicking elsewhere.*

Eventually he shows up, Delilah plays hard-to-get until he tells her the secret of his strength, whereupon she whistles up the Palestinians lurking nearby, who grab him and give him a fetching razor-cut.

Act III *In prison, Samson is the subject of much carping by his fellow inmates. He is then produced as the star attraction in the Palestinian temple, and is a big hit.*

STRANGE BUT TRUE
Samson was first produced by Franz Liszt in Weimar because the Paris Opera still banned biblical subjects on stage, just like Covent Garden, where the first (concert) performance was rather spoiled when the French chorus walked out upon learning that they were expected to sing in English.

NOT MANY PEOPLE KNOW THAT
At the eventual French première (Rouen, 1890) the show was such a hit that part of Act II had to be encored at the end – with the audience contemplating the unfortunate chorus and extras still trapped beneath the ruins of the collapsed temple on stage.

WHAT THE CRITICS THOUGHT
"It is the worst, most rubbishy kind of rubbish." (J.F. Runciman)

CRUSH BAR GAMBIT
"The Jewish captivity is obvious code for the Franco-Prussian War and subsequent occupation of Paris in 1870-71, which Saint-Saëns attributes to the effeminate enfeeblement of France during the sensuous excesses of the reign of Napoleon III. France, embodied in Samson, must die before it can throw off the oppressor and be renewed."

RECORDINGS
❖ Chung, Domingo, Meier, Fondary, Courtis, Bastille Opera Chorus and Orchestra (EMI) ❖ Barenboim, Domingo, Obraztsova, Bruson, Lloyd, Thau, Paris Opera Chorus and Orchestra (DG) ❖

Simon Boccanegra

GIUSEPPE VERDI (1857, REVISED 1881)

It's a doge's life!

In short: *A catastrophically estranged Italian family is reunited – just in time.*

MUSIC

The first version of *Boccanegra* was a disaster, and Verdi seamlessly blended new music with old in his rewrite, whose major addition was the council scene, a 20-minute mixture of stunning drama, a rousing patriotic aria, soaring reconciliation music and a chilling climax as the villain is made to condemn himself. This is a solemn, grown-up and consistently wonderful score, pervaded by beautiful sea-music of gently rocking strings and flittering woodwind. Simon's nobility, Fiesco's wounded grandeur and Paolo's sheer nastiness are brought out in ensembles of immense power: some of this sounds more like *Boris Godunov* than Italian opera.

WORDS

One of those libretti that heroically rises above explaining anything at all. Taken from a play by Gutiérrez, the 1857 words were by Piave and the 1881 revision by Boito.

PLOT

Prelude 1347. *Genoa is suffering class strife. Paolo, a top pleb, fixes the vote so his man Simon, a retired pirate, becomes Doge. Simon reluctantly accepts, thinking it'll mean he'll be allowed to marry the nob Maria, with whom he has a daughter (now vanished). Alas, Maria has just copped it, and her father Fiesco swears to get Simon if it's the last thing he does.*

Act I 1364. *Fiesco, along with various other nobs, has been exiled and is living chez Grimaldi (the Monte Carlo bunch) as guardian to Amelia. Simon has promised her to Paolo for services rendered, but she's set on Gabriele, another exile. It turns out that she is not a Grimaldi at all but – surprise! – Simon's long-lost daughter. Stupidly, they fail to publicise this, but Simon lets her off* *marrying Paolo, who he clearly thinks is a creep. So Paolo arranges to have her kidnapped, and he too swears to get Simon...*

Back in Genoa a council meeting is interrupted by a riot. The kidnap has gone pear-shaped and in the confusion Gabriele and Fiesco (who is of course Amelia's grandfather, though he doesn't know it, yet) are arrested. Paolo is put in charge of the investigation, though everyone knows he did it.

Act II *That evening, Paolo slips some slow poison into Simon's g&t, then tells Gabriele that Simon and Amelia are shacking up together: Gabriele goes crazy, then looks a bit silly when he learns the truth. At this point a short civil war breaks out, organised by Fiesco.*

Act III *It doesn't last long: Simon wins. But the poison is beginning to kick in and he just has time to sort out his differences with Fiesco and apprise him of all outstanding family relationships before he checks out.*

Don't ask

Why on earth does Paolo try to get Gabriele and Fiesco to kill Simon after he's already poisoned him? He can't have forgotten already?

What the critics said

"Monotonous and cold." (Verdi)

Crush Bar gambit

"The rewrite was obviously prompted by the 1878 success of *HMS Pinafore*, and *Boccanegra* is Verdi's attempt at a traditional social comedy. It is patently unthinkable for Gabriele to marry the changeling Amelia if she's a pleb, but the social order is safely restored when her patrician Fiesco ancestry is revealed. Simon, with his unsubstantiated naval past, is clearly modelled on Sir Joseph Porter."

Recording

❖ Abbado, Cappuccilli, Freni, Carreras, Ghiaurov, van Dam, La Scala Chorus and Orchestra (DG) ❖

La Sonnambula

Vincenzo Bellini (1831)

Walking on thin ice!

In short: *A bloke named Elvino narrowly avoids taking over the local pub, which seems a shame.*

Music

Bellini can break all the rules of the theatre – such as providing a drama in which nothing happens for the first half-hour – but you forgive him as soon as he spins out one of his lovely lazy tunes, with which this most affecting of his operas abounds: particularly Amina's melting *Come per me sereno*, as well as her reef-strewn sleepwalking scene and final burst of joyful coloratura in *Ah non giunge*. The range of emotion conveyed in these and her equally beautiful duets with Elvino make her one of the more rounded of romantic heroines. Act I finishes with a tremendous, slow-building quartet with a thundering dramatic conclusion as Elvino calls off the wedding, and there is some wonderful instrumental writing (belying Bellini's reputation as a hobbled orchestrator) as Rodolfo gives his lecture on somnambulism.

Words

Originally a vaudeville by Eugène Scribe, who then turned this extended anecdote into a ballet with Hérold. Felice Romani knocked out the libretto when his previous project with Bellini ran into trouble with the censor.

Plot

Act I We are in Switzerland, and it is Amina and Elvino's wedding day, a cause for rejoicing for all except local innkeeper Lisa, Elvino's ex. A toff, Rodolfo, arrives and starts pawing Amina, to Elvino's alarm, then puts up at the inn where he has a crack at Lisa too. This is interrupted by the arrival of the sleepwalking Amina. With heroic restraint Rodolfo controls his urge to rape her. She racks out on his sofa, and he hops it through the window in order to avoid embarrassment in front of the peasants who have found out that he is the long-absent lord of the manor and have come to do some toadying. Elvino appears and breaks off the engagement.

Act II *Elvino plans to take advantage of the fact that he's booked the church and marry Lisa, despite Rodolfo's assurances that "nothing happened". Luckily at the last moment Amina puts in an appearance doing a high-wire sleep-walk on the roof, and the grudging yokels accept that her behaviour is the result of a psychological disturbance other than nymphomania.*

DON'T ASK

This Amina seems to sleep at very odd times of day. Is she narcoleptic, as well?

FANCY THAT

Sullivan made two of his best parodies – *A nice dilemma* from *Trial by Jury* and *Carefully on tiptoe stealing* from *Pirates* – out of the Act I finale.

WHAT THE PAPERS SAID

"He is merely an imitator. But for Rossini he would never have existed as a composer. Rossini would cut up into a thousand such." (*The Examiner*)

CRUSH BAR GAMBIT

"There are some pretty sinister things going on in this village: notice how Elvino visits his mother's grave and reappears *with her wedding ring*. It is also clear enough that the cut-price Casanova Rodolfo, intent on reviving *droit de seigneur*, is Amina's long-lost father, and it is his mauling of her that induces her hysterical somnambulism. Memories from the past? A case for the police, I think."

RECORDINGS

❖ Bonynge, Sutherland, Pavarotti, Jones, Ghiaurov, London Opera Chorus, National Philharmonic (Decca) ❖ Votto, Callas, Monti, Cossotto, Zaccaria, Ratti, La Scala (EMI: mono) ❖

The Tales of Hoffmann

JACQUES OFFENBACH (1880)

He found his true love – in his cups!

In short: *An inebriated writer misses the second half of an opera and his rendezvous with the prima donna.*

MUSIC

A happy marriage of his insouciant muse with fantastic Romanticism, Offenbach's only true opera feels more German than French thanks to the atmosphere of Hoffmann's stories and a fair sprinkling of *Student Prince*-style choruses. Unlike his operettas there is no pastiche, the rousing songs and set-pieces are interspersed with moments of high passion, and the music restores some of Hoffmann's magic to a schematic libretto. Like his idol Mozart, Offenbach found it hard to write a dull note and knew the virtues of harmonic restraint; he has a highly engaging way with a tune, orchestrates prettily, and writes fiendish coloratura for the poor soprano. Showstoppers: the thumping drinking songs of the prelude; Olympia's bravura *Les oiseaux dans la charmille*; the barcarolle, star of many a TV ad; Hoffmann's duets with Giulietta – Puccini without the hysterics – and Antonia, a sweet piece of wistful melancholia.

WORDS

By Jules Barbier after the 1851 play he co-wrote with Michel Carré based loosely on stories by E.T.A. Hoffmann.

PLOT

Prelude *In a pub next door to the Nuremberg opera house everyone is sitting out the second act of* Don Giovanni. *Hoffmann, awaiting a tryst with the soprano Stella after the show, passes time by reliving his disastrous love affairs. The saturnine Lindorf, who has an unexplained but obviously sizeable grudge against Hoffmann, has his own plans for Stella.*

Act I *Hoffmann buys some unreliable spectacles from Coppelius (Lindorf in another guise) and falls in love with Olympia, foolishly failing to notice that she is a robot. Following a contractual dispute with Olympia's maker, Coppelius smashes her to bits.*

Act II *Hoffmann's next girlfriend is Antonia, a consumptive singer who urgently needs to give up singing before it kills her. Dr Miracle (guess who) persuades her to have a last warble. She has a seizure and dies.*

Act III *Hoffmann tries his luck with Giulietta, a Venetian prostitute. Sadly she is in league with Dapertutto (him again) and sweet-talks Hoffmann into giving her his reflection. A bit thirsty after her exertions, she carelessly drinks some poison intended for a third party.*

Epilogue *Hoffmann, pretty drunk by now, decides to give up women. Stella appears from the opera house, takes one look at him and heads off with Lindorf.*

DIRECTORIAL PRESUMPTION
For the first (posthumous) performance, Carvalho, head of the Paris Opéra-Comique, ditched the third act, moved the second to Venice to accommodate the barcarolle, turned the dialogue into recit and threw out the epilogue quartet.

WHAT WAGNER THOUGHT
"He possesses the warmth Auber lacks – but it is the warmth of the dungheap."

CRUSH BAR GAMBIT
"It is a fable of gender incompatibility. Hoffmann's idealisation of women either unsexes them or, in the case of Giulietta, results in his own metaphorical castration. Stella, the eternal feminine, will desert the artist and sell her soul to the devil. The depressing conclusion is that men prefer drinking and women prefer jewels."

RECORDINGS
❖ Bonynge, Domingo, Sutherland, Bacquier, Suisse Romande Chorus and Orchestra (Decca) ❖ Nagano, Alagna, Jo, van Dam, Lyons Opera Chorus and Orchestra (Erato) ❖

Tannhäuser

RICHARD WAGNER (1845, REVISED 1861)

It's a bloomin' miracle!

In short: *A singing knight fails to persuade his friends of the joys of carnality.*

MUSIC

There is some disparity between the conviction of Venus's swooning sensuality and the phoney piety of the Wartburg (the sort of stuff that made the likes of this and *Faust* so popular with the Victorians). A curious mixture of Rossinian cabaletta-forms and Wagner's early attempts to create a continuous music-drama, *Tannhäuser* contains some wondrous stuff: the overture, with its pompous pilgrim music, shades directly into Venus's impossible hedonism, Tannhäuser's Venus-song crops up repeatedly, Elisabeth says hallo to the competition venue very prettily, and Wolfram's *Star of eve* is an entertaining piece of schmaltz. The Parisian première of the rewrite was a notable disaster.

WORDS

A cut-and-paste job of mediaeval tales, namely the legend of Tannhäuser and the Pope's fecund pole, the singing contests in the Wartburg (not the East German automobile but a castle near Eisenach) and the story of St Elisabeth. Typically, Wagner wanted to call it *The Mount of Venus*.

PLOT

Act I *Heinrich, aka Tannhäuser, has been having a whale of a time chez Venus inside a mountain but is hankering after the open spaces. You'll come crawling back, says Venus, and vanishes. Back in the open spaces Heinrich has a religious frenzy as some pilgrims wander past, and is discovered by his pals the musical knights from the Wartburg (residence of local bigwig Hermann) who take him home.*

Act II *Hermann's niece Elisabeth is pretty glad to hear Heinrich's back. There is about to be a sort of Eurovision contest, sadly restricted to German competitors – the prize being Elisabeth. Heinrich starts warbling on about the* *joy of sex, causing an uproar – indeed only Elisabeth's timely intervention saves him from being skewered. The general consensus is that he should go off to Rome and ask the Pope to forgive him. He goes.*

Act III *When Heinrich fails to return with the other pilgrims Elisabeth hauls off and dies – foolishly, since he turns up five minutes later. He explains how the Pope said he had as much chance of being saved as his staff had of bursting into flower, and reckons he might as well go back to Venus. Instead, he dies, and a second wave of pilgrims appear with the news that the Pope's staff is now sprouting quite nicely.*

DON'T ASK
These singing knights, I suppose they're a bit like Sir Cliff Richard and Sir Elton John, then?

SCRATCH YER EYES OUT
Offenbach "borrowed" the pre-competition fanfare for *La Belle Hélène*; in a possibly connected move, Wagner described the latter as "full of a Jew's hatred towards the Greece of marble temples and oleanders".

WHAT ROSSINI THOUGHT
"One needs to hear this music more than once. I won't be going again."

CRUSH BAR GAMBIT
"*Tannhäuser* is a satire on the operatic obsession with female virginity. Wagner wittily turns the usual state of affairs upside down, and has Tannhäuser committing unforgivable pre-marital sins of the flesh. Sadly one suspects Wagner was motivated less by proto-feminist outrage than by a need to find some way of preventing this marriage between non-blood relations."

RECORDINGS
❖ Solti, Kollo, Dernesch, Ludwig, Sotin, Braun, Vienna State Opera Chorus, Vienna Philharmonic (Decca) ❖ Konwitschny, Hopf, Grummer, Fischer, Schech, Frick, Wunderlich, Berlin State Opera Chorus and Orchestra (EMI) ❖

The Threepenny Opera

KURT WEILL (1928)

Crime pays!

In short: *A well-connected nogoodnik is ennobled.*

MUSIC

Weill perfected the Berlin cabaret idiom in his play-with-songs in much
the same way as this musical chameleon did with his largely (and unjustly)
forgotten Broadway musicals. Sustained by memorably insinuating tunes,
the genius of *Threepenny Opera* lies in his use of mock-naïve, parodic pop-
music – a blend of vamping night-club tunes, ragtime, tango, foxtrot and
even a Lutheran hymn – to heighten the sheer cynicism and disgust of what
is being sung. The atmosphere of off-colour nostalgia is emphasised by
Weill's cleverly "wrong" harmonies and schmoozy saxophones. Its biggest hit,
The Ballad of Mac the Knife, was composed as an afterthought.

WORDS

An updating to Dickensian London of John Gay's 1728 *Beggar's Opera* by the
writing team formerly known as Bertolt Brecht. Gay's work had been revived
in London in 1920 and was a huge hit; Brecht's collaborator Elisabeth
Hauptmann translated the book, and Bert probably wrote the lyrics (the
ones he didn't nick from François Villon and Rudyard Kipling, anyway).

PLOT

Act I *Jonathan Peachum, purveyor of beggars' accoutrements, is disappointed
to learn that his daughter Polly has gone and married Captain Macheath
(aka Mac the Knife), a gangster, and decides to shop him for the £40 reward.*

Act II *Polly tells Mac he might like to make himself scarce for a while.
However, Mrs Peachum, knowing Mac's weakness for the company of
prostitutes, bribes some of them to turn him in. Sure enough Mac visits the*

brothel and is picked up by the cops – particularly galling for him as the police chief, Tiger Brown, is an old mate with whom he has assiduously shared his earnings. Happily, Brown's daughter Lucy, an old flame of Mac's, springs him from Old Bailey.

Act III Peachum threatens to disrupt Queen Victoria's coronation by flooding the streets with beggars unless Brown gets his act together and has Mac hanged. Mac is picked up with the whores again. Luckily, as he is about to step onto the gallows, a royal messenger arrives with a pardon and a peerage.

NAZI NOTES

The score was displayed, like that of Berg's *Wozzeck*, at the *Degenerate Music* exhibition in Dusseldorf in 1938, helpfully annotated to highlight the especially corrupt parts. The booth where visitors could listen to Bert 'n' Kurt's Commie propaganda was unaccountably popular.

WHAT THE PAPERS SAID

"All very crude and painful." (*Musical Times*)

PRODUCTION BLUES

Mrs Peachum refused to sing *The Ballad of Sexual Dependency* or indeed to take part in "this filthy play"; Polly dropped out a week before the première to look after her dying husband; the madam's part was cut when she got appendicitis; and Peter Lorre had to be replaced as Peachum at the last minute. The final dress rehearsal went on for 16 hours.

CRUSH BAR GAMBIT

"*Threepenny Opera* demonstrates the drawbacks of being too *engagé*: whereas the light touch of Gay's satire started the process that brought down the Walpole government, Brecht's self-consciously left-wing revolutionary posing had the opposite effect, and merely fuelled the rise of the Nazi party, whose petty-bourgeois supporters saw themselves in the victimised Macheath."

RECORDINGS
❖ Brückner-Rüggeberg, Lenya, Neuss, Trenk-Trebisch, Hesterberg, Schellow, Kóczián, Chorus and Dance Orchestra of Radio Free Berlin (Sony) ❖ Mauceri, Kollo, Lemper, Milva, Adorf, Dernesch, Berlin RIAS Chamber Choir and Sinfonia (Decca) ❖

Tosca

GIACOMO PUCCINI (1900)

The high-diving diva!

In short: *An over-emotional singer causes the deaths of her lover, a freedom fighter, a policeman and herself in the course of an eventful night.*

MUSIC
Even those who loathe *Tosca* tend to admit that this brazen assault on the emotions achieves its aims most efficiently (as Shostakovich said: "Puccini writes marvellous operas but dreadful music"). Strong meat from the crashing opening chords onwards, the torture episode can be pretty unbearable; but it is also Puccini's most tuneful work (including *Vissi d'arte, E lucevan le stelle, O dolci mani*), his most atmospheric (he spent a night on the roof of Castel Sant'Angelo to write down the noises of Rome waking up for the beginning of Act III), and has one of opera's most satisfying villains – see the unsubtle but thrilling Act I finale as Scarpia roars out his impious creed against the choir's thunderous *Te Deum*.

WORDS
Blood and thunder from a play by Victorien Sardou, set in the final days of the Bourbon monarchy in Rome in 1800, with an overt emphasis on sex and sadism. (Angelotti is probably based on the Neapolitan rebel Caracciolo, whom Nelson strung from his yardarm.) The operatic rights belonged to one Franchetti; Puccini persuaded him an opera would never work and then snapped up the rights as soon as Franchetti dropped them.

PLOT
Act I *Cavaradossi, an atheist painter rather surprisingly working on a portrait of Mary Magdalene, hides Angelotti, a political prisoner on the lam, in a well in his garden. The sensationally unpleasant copper on the case, Scarpia, who fancies Cavaradossi's girlfriend, Tosca, has her followed to track down the fugitive, but nobody looks down the well.*

Act II *Cavaradossi is arrested and tortured. Tosca is invited to attend, and spills the beans. Scarpia offers her Cavaradossi's life – via a staged execution.– in exchange for a quickie. She agrees but rather unfairly stabs him before he can accomplish the deed.*

Act III *Tosca scoots off to the Castel Sant'Angelo for the fake execution which – surprise! – turns out to be real. Scarpia's murder is discovered and Tosca takes the high road over the battlements to her death.*

BEST DISASTER
In San Francisco in 1961 a badly-briefed firing squad shot Tosca instead of Cavaradossi and then, having been told to "exit with the principals", followed her over the battlements.

NOT MANY PEOPLE KNOW THAT
Old Soviet productions – where a happy ending was *de rigueur*, just like in real Russian life – renamed the opera *The Struggle for Communism*, Cavaradossi's fresco was of the Red Army and there was a *real* fake execution: Cavaradossi then bounced to his feet and headed off into the sunset (well, sunrise) with Tosca.

WHAT THE PAPERS SAID
"Coarsely puerile, pretentious and vapid." (*Mercure de France*)

CRUSH BAR GAMBIT
"Tosca's doom – and everyone else's – is entirely a result of her fatal, schizoid combination of religious dementia and uncontrolled nymphomania. The jealousy that leads the police to Angelotti is an inverted projection of the guilt associated with her sinful relationship with the irreligious Cavaradossi. Her subsequent betrayal of Cavaradossi and Angelotti makes Scarpia her confessor: no wonder she finds it difficult to have sex with him."

RECORDINGS
❖ de Sabata, Callas, Gobbi, di Stefano, La Scala (EMI)
❖ Davis, Caballé, Carreras, Wixell, Covent Garden (Philips) ❖

La Traviata

Giuseppe Verdi (1853)

Time to cough up!

In short: *A spell in the country fails to cure a consumptive* poule de luxe.

Music

Verdi's best-loved opera was written more or less simultaneously with
Il trovatore. It is his most intimate work, basically a three-hander, and the
first serious opera to take a contemporary subject, though the censor weirdly
insisted on a Louis XIV dress code. *Traviata* has an unstoppable flow of
gorgeous tunes, and Violetta's destruction – as much by social attitudes as
her disease – is painfully pointed by the music, notably the washed-out
violins that begin the prelude and last act. The score is dominated by
strings, some of the lines as long as Bellini's but with an inimitably Verdian
expressiveness. Highlights come in huge chunks: the whole of Act I, as
flighty Violetta is won over by Alfredo; her wrenching Act II duet with
Germont; Alfredo's fury and remorse; and her pathetic death.

Words

From Dumas's *La dame aux camélias*, a semi-autobiographical tale of his
youthful fling with a sickly courtesan (the title refers to her habit of wearing
a red camellia on those days of the month when she was "not available").
Verdi probably saw the play in Paris in 1852, and Piave wrote the libretto.

Plot

Act I *Alfredo has a crush on Violetta, a top-dollar call-girl with dicky lungs,
and persuades her to fall in love with him (cheaper that way).*

Act II *They shack up in bucolic bliss for a while, with Violetta footing the
bills (without Alfredo's knowledge), but Alfredo's father Mr Germont puts in a
request for her to vacate the scene so his daughter can contract an advantageous
marriage. Improbably, she complies, and hitches up with her ex (fast work!)
for a party at her friend Flora's that evening. Alfredo, unaware of daddy's
intervention, waylays her at the said party, thrashes the ex at an unspecified*

card game and furiously pays Violetta off with the winnings, eliciting widespread opprobrium. He also gets into a duel with the ex.

Act III Weeks later, Violetta is dying. The ex is nowhere to be seen. Alfredo, who is finally up to speed, shows up. Too late. She dies.

DON'T ASK
Hey, Mr Germont, who invited you to Flora's party?

TWO FAT LADIES
Traviata has been dogged by a perceived incongruity between some prima donnas and the consumptive they portray, notably the "considerable" (20st 7lb) Fanny Salvini-Donatelli, who created the role, and Luisa Tetrazzini: John McCormack described the experience of lifting her off the bed in Act III as like "fondling a pair of Michelin tyres".

WHAT THE PAPERS SAID
"Trashy ... a prurient story prettily acted." (*Athenaeum*)

CRUSH BAR GAMBIT
"*Traviata* is an economic primer about the fiscal nature of human relationships and the value of women as commercial assets. Violetta's crime is to disrupt the monogamous family as economic entity, which as Engels pointed out is primarily a mechanism for keeping property intact. Her job represents the subversive tendency of property to circulate without vesting, endemic to *laissez-faire* systems."

RECORDINGS
❖ Giulini, Callas, di Stefano, Bastianini, La Scala (EMI)
❖ Solti, Gheorghiu, Lopardo, Nucci, Covent Garden (Decca) ❖

Tristan and Isolde

RICHARD WAGNER (1865)

Ocean potion – poisoned passion!

In short: *French interference in Anglo-Irish relations results in disaster for all concerned.*

MUSIC

The most extreme of operas, the apotheosis and the beginning of the end of Romanticism, doing more to destroy diatonic tonality than any other work. The famous suspensions of the prelude only find their resolution four hours later in Isolde's even better-known orgasmic death scene. An immensely long love song of uncontrolled passion, it has a dense, lush, chromatic score and requires two singers of preternatural stamina to get through it. The first of Wagner's seamless music-dramas, its interior nature is reflected in his amazing interweaving of motifs to convey moods. Tough to pick out individual high-lights, but Isolde's *Liebestod* is surely the most shattering of operatic finales.

WORDS

From the Celtic legend, via a 13th-century poem by Gottfried von Strassburg. Tristan's wife, another Isolde, is wisely edited out.

PLOT

Morold, an Irish giant terrorising Cornwall, has been killed by Tristan, a Breton mercenary and nephew of Cornish King Mark. Tristan's wounds were treated by Isolde, an aristocratic Irish nurse who, to complicate matters, was formerly engaged to Morold. Now Tristan has gone to fetch Isolde to marry Mark in furtherance of the Anglo-Irish truce.

Act I *On the boat from Ireland to Cornwall. Isolde is pissed off with Tristan: not only has he murdered her fiancé (and sent her his head in a box), she is now in love with him and is far from keen to marry Mark. She decides to kill Tristan – missed her chance earlier, really – and commit suicide by drinking poison. But in a hilarious mix-up they both take some Viagra that Isolde's* *mother has given her to get the ageing Mark through his wedding night. This puts them into a permanent frenzy of lust.*

Act II *Tristan and Isolde meet by moonlight while Mark and co are out hunting, and are caught more or less in the act. Tristan is injured in the ensuing scuffle.*

Act III *Back in Brittany, Tristan convalesces noisily. Isolde arrives and he immediately dies. Isolde's heart also packs up after she sings some very high notes, very loud.*

Don't ask
What on earth is Mark hunting for in the middle of the night? Bats?

What the critics said
"The prelude reminds me of the old Italian painting of a martyr whose intestines are slowly unwound from his body on a reel." (Eduard Hanslick)

Unique selling point
Contains absolutely no Germans.

Fatal statistics
In addition to the onstage death-count (four), this most dangerous of operas has accounted for the first Tristan, Ludwig Carolsfeld (replacing George Ander, who went mad), who died shortly after the premiere; Felix Mottl and Joseph Keilberth, who pegged out conducting the second act; and Wagner's father-in-law Franz Liszt, who collapsed in Act III, dying soon after.

Crush Bar gambit
"Tristan, like Siegfried, can feel sexual attraction only towards members of his immediate family, in this case going so far as to make Isolde his aunt before being able to sleep with her. These skewed Oedipal urges have much to do with Wagner's denial of his own bastardy and rejection of his real father's ethnically dubious name, Geyer."

Recordings
❖ Böhm, Windgassen, Nilsson, Bayreuth Festival Chorus and Orchestra (DG) ❖ Karajan, Vickers, Dernesch, Berlin Philharmonic Orchestra (EMI) ❖

Il Trovatore

Giuseppe Verdi (1853)

Burn, baby, burn!

In short: A man goes to extreme lengths to silence an itinerant busker.

Music

Inspired by his demented characters, Verdi produced the last word in *bel canto* melodrama: *Di quella pira*, the Anvil Chorus and *Squilli, echeggi la tromba* are the essence of Italian opera. Not awfully subtle, but it provides full-blooded music at unprecedented pace. Absolute highlights are the Act II finale, including Luna's civilisedly passionate *Il balen del suo sorriso*, and the beginning of Act IV, as Leonora and Manrico serenade each other desperately from either side of the prison walls while a bevy of monks gloomily intones a *Miserere*. As Caruso noted, it just needs the four greatest singers in the world.

Words

By Salvatore Cammarano and Leone Bardare from a play by Garcia Gutiérrez, this power struggle among sacrilegious, vindictive, doomed erotomaniacs set in 15th-century Spain might be a mission-statement for opera.

Plot

20 years ago The Count of Luna spots a gypsy hanging around his baby son Garcia, who develops a cold, so he has the gypsy incinerated. Her daughter, Azucena, kidnaps Garcia. Later, the remains of a child are found in the embers …

Act I The new Count of Luna (other son of the above) finds his pursuit of the desirable Leonora thwarted by a mysterious troubadour who has taken to howling outside her window. The three of them bump into each other in the garden; Luna finds out that the howler is one Manrico, a well-known insurgent, and picks a fight.

Act II Manrico, who won the duel but omitted to polish Luna off, is back in the mountains with his old ma – guess who: Azucena. She raves on about her mother, raising serious doubts as to whether it was Garcia or her own child that she chucked on the bonfire in all the excitement. Manrico (no rocket scientist) fails to make the obvious connection, ie, that he is Luna's brother. Leonora, who thinks Manrico is dead, is about to take the veil. Both Luna and Manrico turn up to stop her. She heads off with Manrico.

Act III Manrico and co are being besieged by Luna, whose men arrest a gypsy they find looking at them in a funny way: Azucena, of course. She is sentenced to burn. Manrico rides out to the rescue …

Act IV … and fails: both he and Azucena are now in the slammer. Leonora offers herself to Luna in exchange for Manrico's release, then takes poison. She dies. Luna has Manrico's head chopped off and forces Azucena to watch – at which inappropriate moment she reveals that Manrico was his brother.

WHAT DICKENS THOUGHT
"It seemed rubbish on the whole to me."

BLUE PENCIL NOTES
The frequent mentions of "the stake" were cut by order of the Papal censor, in case people were reminded of the Inquisition.

CRUSH BAR GAMBIT
"Leonora's suspicious freedom of movement between the two sides suggests she is a Mata Hari figure in the pay of government forces. In fact the consistent skill with which she manipulates the situation to Manrico's disadvantage, while managing to avoid either becoming a nun or marrying him, makes her eventual fate seem particularly heroic."

RECORDINGS
❖ Karajan, Corelli, Price, Vienna State Opera Chorus, Vienna Philharmonic (DG: live) ❖ Mehta, Domingo, Price, Ambrosian Opera Chorus, New Philharmonia (RCA) ❖

Turandot

GIACOMO PUCCINI (1926)

He came, he thawed, he conquered!

In short: *A chilly Chinese princess with homicidal tendencies is won over to the attractions of the male sex by a Man With No Name.*

MUSIC

Puccini's last opera, and his most adventurous, combining the drama of *Tosca*, the sentimentality of *Bohème* and the comedy of *Gianni Schicchi* with better exoticism than *Butterfly*. The orchestra bristles with gongs, glockenspiels, celesta, xylophone and drums, and there is an effective mixture of the Chinese and the Italian. The jokey *chinoiserie* of the three Masks (lifted from *commedia dell'arte*) provides light relief from the encircling gloom, and the chorus is stirringly used to produce elemental crowd scenes. Puccini died in the middle of composing Act III and Franco Alfano's completion, while not bad, fails to make as much of the final love duet as Puccini might have done. Showstoppers: Act I begins with a chilling mob scene and ends with a classic Puccini crescendo, the entire company weighing in over repeating harmonies; Liù's rather gratuitous death adds the necessary pathos and *Nessun dorma*, one of Puccini's noblest arias, has enough class to survive any amount of abuse.

WORDS

By Giuseppe Adami and Renato Simoni, who took the story from the 18th-century Venetian playwright and *commedia dell'arte* fan Carlo Gozzi, via an Italian translation of a German version by Schiller. Liù, one of those Puccinian women who dies futilely for love, was the composer's own invention.

PLOT

Act I *Peking, some time back, and it's execution time for Princess Turandot's latest suitor, who has unsatisfactorily answered a number of riddles set by the princess. She seems pretty keen not to marry: this is the ninety-ninth of her admirers to get the chop. Among the audience are Calaf (a wandering Tartar* *prince) and a slave-girl, Liù, who is pointlessly besotted with Calaf. Calaf inappropriately decides he's in love with Turandot and announces same in time-honoured fashion by banging a gong.*

Act II *Some palace lackeys lament Turandot's psychotic behaviour; she explains that she is simply avenging the rape and murder of a distant ancestress. Calaf solves Turandot's riddles, much to her dismay, then in a surprise move says he will agree to be executed anyway if she can find out his name before dawn.*

Act III *Which turns out to have been a silly thing to do, as Liù is now subjected to torture in an attempt to get her to reveal Calaf's name. She kills herself to avoid further unpleasantness. Dawn arrives. Calaf gives Turandot a quick kiss, and she decides he's not so bad after all.*

NOT MANY PEOPLE KNOW THAT
Puccini pinched the Emperor's fanfare from Frederick Norton's 1916 musical comedy *Chu Chin Chow*.

STRANGE BUT TRUE
The composer's original plan with Adami and Simoni was to write an opera based on *Oliver Twist*, tentatively entitled *Fanny*.

CRUSH BAR GAMBIT
"As the Masks helpfully point out, Turandot does not in fact exist: she is a subconscious psychosexual fantasy conjured by Puccini's proto-Oedipal neurosis. *Eros* and *thanatos* were indivisible, particularly as far as his women are concerned: Liù must die, like all his previous heroines, because of her love for Calaf. It was logically impossible for Puccini to create a happy ending, so the only option left was for him to die as well."

RECORDINGS
❖ Mehta, Sutherland, Pavarotti, Caballé, London Philharmonic Orchestra (Decca) ❖ Serafin, Callas, Fernandi, Schwarzkopf, La Scala Chorus and Orchestra (EMI) ❖

The Turn of the Screw

BENJAMIN BRITTEN (1954)

Just dying to be of service!

In short: *Two servants refuse to leave their posts, notwithstanding the fact that they are dead, with unfortunate results.*

WORDS

Myfanwy Piper (wife of John, who produced the scenery for the first performance at La Fenice) deftly adapted Henry James's novelette, making it more sinister, if less ambiguous, than the original. There is little doubt about the reality of the ghosts (who do not speak in the book), nor of the nature of their influence on the children.

MUSIC

A laconic masterpiece for six singers and an orchestra of 13, composed in four months for the 1954 Venice Biennale. Two introductory piano arpeggios evoke the fusty Jamesian world. The opera is divided into 15 scenes, each preceded by increasingly tense variations on a theme – the screw being turned. The sung music also revolves around very few themes, variously treated: the ghosts' music is both literally haunting and exotically alluring; when Quint calls Miles's name it sounds like a muezzin's call to prayer. The children slip from nursery rhyme chants to strange melancholy invocations of the ghosts. The governess gets lost in a labyrinth of jangly hysteria.

PLOT

Act I *A nameless governess in charge of two orphaned children, Miles and Flora, is bothered by a strange man. The housekeeper tells her it is Peter Quint, a former valet. Further, and unsettlingly, the governess also learns that he is dead, and that he took unspecified liberties with Miles while alive. Quint is* shortly joined by the equally deceased Miss Jessel, a previous governess, whom Quint apparently drove to her death. The children begin to behave oddly.

Act II The ghosts discuss their evil designs on the children. The governess writes for help to the children's guardian, but Miles pinches the letter. The housekeeper takes Flora away after she is found wandering in the garden with Miss J. The governess tries to force the truth out of Miles, who – a bit of a surprise – keels over and dies.

STRANGE BUT TRUE
Commuters will be pleased to know that Britten composed part of the opera – the 13-part fugue – on the train from Ipswich to Liverpool Street.

ESPIONAGE CONNECTION
Britten, who had been at the same school as Donald Maclean, was questioned by police in 1953 following Maclean's defection to Moscow, as the Home Secretary began "a new drive against male vice".

DON'T ASK
Whatever happened to David Hemmings, the original Miles and future star of such cinematic masterpieces as *Beyond Erotica* and *Just a Gigolo*?

WHAT THE PAPERS SAID
"It is an improper question for criticism to ask, but it [homosexuality] recurs so invariably that it must have some relevance to his art." (*The Times*)

CRUSH BAR GAMBIT
"*The Turn of The Screw* is the most astonishing exposition of paedophiliac psychosis in opera. The boy Miles is a kind of invert Lolita: it is he who lures Quint, a typical paederast fantasy. The rejection of female sexuality is wholesale: Quint deserts Miss Jessel for Miles, who in turn rebuffs the governess, indeed goes so far as to die to escape her clutches. In the end hers is the only innocence to be corrupted."

RECORDINGS
❖ Britten, Vyvyan, Dyer, Pears, Hemmings, English Opera Group Orchestra (London) ❖ Bedford, Lott, Pay, Hube, Langridge, Aldeburgh Festival Ensemble (Collins) ❖

Werther

JULES MASSENET (1892)

He missed his aim – twice!

In short: *A young woman spares the world some drippy poetry by driving her rejected lover to suicide.*

MUSIC

For some reason people have always had it in for poor old Massenet: even during his lifetime he was known as "Gounod's daughter". *Werther* floats along on a stream of well-mannered, short-breathed melodies and wonderful scoring, rising at times to quite dramatic heights but essentially civilised, restrained sensuality. The bourgeois contentment of small-town German life is perfectly captured, Werther and Charlotte's love-music develops magically from remembered party themes into a big romantic string tune, Werther's desperation boils over in his angst-ridden *J'aurais sur ma poitrine*, Sophie's jolly tunes are full of chirruping woodwind, Charlotte reads Werther's letters to a haunting sax, and the final scenes produce a real proto-Puccinian frisson.

WORDS

From Goethe's epistolary novel of 1774, which set off the literary movement known as *Sturm und Drang* and a spate of copycat suicides (about which the author commented: "If there are fools who take harm from reading it, dammit! – so much the worse for them"). Libretto by Edouard Blau, Paul Milliet and Georges Hartmann.

PLOT

Act I Wetzlar, near Frankfurt, July 1780-ish. Werther, a poet (25), presents himself at the local magistrate's house to take his daughter Charlotte, 20, on a blind date to the local bash. Afterwards they wander around amorously gazing at stars, etc. Suddenly Charlotte remembers that she has a fiancé, Albert, who is just due back from a business trip. This upsets Werther: he threatens to kill himself.

Act II *September. Charlotte is married, and Werther is still eating himself up about it (but not dead). Albert offers him some comforting words, Charlotte suggests he goes away till Christmas. No, for ever! says W, threatening to kill himself.*

Act III *Christmas Eve. Charlotte gets emotional reading Werther's letters and her little sister Sophie comforts her. Werther appears, having obviously decided to spoil Christmas for everyone. Charlotte finally admits she loves him – then immediately sends him away again. Werther sends a note asking whether he might borrow Albert's pistols. No problemo, says Albert.*

Act IV *Charlotte runs over to Werther's place. He has shot himself, but (no marksman) is still alive. However, he dies about 20 minutes later.*

STRANGE BUT TRUE

Werther was rejected by the Opéra-Comique, whose director called it "depressing" and said it was "doomed from the start". The next day his theatre burned down, and the opera was finally premièred in Vienna.

WHAT DEBUSSY THOUGHT

"A master in the art of pandering to stupid ideas and cheap amateur standards."

CRUSH BAR GAMBIT

"*Werther* is notable for the dawning of self-awareness in operatic characters. Charlotte and Sophia hound poor Werther to death as gender-revenge for the legions of dead operatic heroines. They conspire to drive him mad, confusing the preternaturally sensitive nature poet by singing Christmas carols in June and spring songs in September, praising the poetaster Klopstock and forcing him to observe Charlotte's marital bliss."

RECORDINGS

❖ Davis, von Stade, Carreras, Allen, Buchanan, Lloyd, Children's Chorus, Covent Garden (Philips) ❖ Cohen, Vallin, Thill, Roque, Féraldy, Narçon, Niel, Cantoria Children's Choir, Opéra-Comique Chorus and Orchestra (EMI: mono, 1931 recording) ❖

William Tell

GIOACHINO ROSSINI (1829)

Swiss on a roll!

In short: *Abuse of fruit sparks a revolution.*

MUSIC

It's worth the effort to adjust to the extremely leisurely pace of Rossini's final opera, a four-hour extravaganza which more or less instituted the French tradition of Grand Opera. From the brilliant four-part overture, an impressionistic résumé of the story, to the glowing *ranz-des-vaches* playout of harps, horns and chorus *Tell* is full of good things and surprising subtleties, scenes expansively built to grand climaxes, duets and ensembles of a passion and drama not to be found again until the later Verdi. Even the longueurs (the Act I choruses and Act III dances) are never less than good listening, and the high points – most of Act II, the apple-shooting, Arnold's *Asile héréditaire* and the lovely swoopy soprano trio with squeezebox accompaniment in Act IV, among others – are truly special.

WORDS

Schiller's 1803 play about the apocryphal 14th-century Swiss patriot adapted by two characters named Bis and Jouy.

PLOT

Act I *During a rustic Swiss cult-style multiple wedding, local patriot William tries to foment revolt against the occupying Austrians, and gives a pep-talk to Arnold, a vacillating character who is secretly in love with one Matilda, an Austrian princess. Tell then rescues a shepherd the Austrians are after, following which the Austrians torch the village and arrest Arnold's old dad.*

Act II *William interrupts Arnold's tête-à-tête with Matilda with the news that his father has been executed. This does the trick. A large number of Swiss rebels get together.*

Act III *Arnold and Matilda agree that in the circumstances their relationship is going nowhere. Gessler, the local Austrian boss, organises a Soviet-style spontaneous demonstration of pro-Austrian enthusiasm, at which Tell steps out of line and is required to go through the old apple-shooting routine with his son Jemmy. Matilda rescues Jemmy, but Tell is arrested and taken away to be fed to reptiles.*

Act IV *Arnold and co set off to start a revolt. Jemmy is reunited with his ma, then Tell appears on the lake with Gessler. There is a storm; somehow Tell manages to escape from the boat and kill Gessler. Word arrives that the revolt has been successful. The weather clears up.*

TENOR TROUBLE
Arnold's role is such a pig that Auguste Laget described *Tell* as "that destructive opera which has exterminated three generations of tenors". First to go was Adolphe Nourrit, who created the role, singing the top notes in the normal (for the time) half-voice; but in 1837 Gilbert Duprez sang it and became the first tenor to belt out the top Cs Pavarotti-style (a noise Rossini called "the squawk of a capon whose throat is being cut"). Nourrit, in the audience, retired on the spot and killed himself two years later.

WHAT THE CRITICS SAID
"Peasants, mountains, miseries." (Rossini)

CRUSH BAR GAMBIT
"The reason Rossini retired from writing operas after *Tell*, at the age of 37, is contained within it. This wistful opera is all about fatherhood, Tell's relationship with Jemmy and Arnold's with his father, and Rossini became obsessed by the thought of his own sexual sterility and consequently unable to compose another note."

RECORDINGS
❖ Chailly, Milnes, Freni, Pavarotti, Ambrosian Opera Chorus, National Philharmonic Orchestra (Decca: in Italian) ❖ Gardelli, Bacquier, Caballé, Gedda, Ambrosian Opera Chorus, Royal Philharmonic Orchestra (EMI) ❖

Wozzeck

ALBAN BERG (1925)

Major cock-up on the domestic front!

In short: *A dyspeptic soldier makes an indigestible mess of his home life.*

MUSIC

It may not be everybody's cup of tea, but the score of *Wozzeck* is fiendishly clever: for example, the postlude to the first scene is a note-for-note repeat of the prelude – backwards. But don't panic. Berg claimed he didn't want anyone to notice *how* the score was built, only to "be filled with the idea of the opera". This spiky, intense music draws you into poor Wozzeck's claustrophobic world of betrayal and paranoia and spits you out the other side considerably chastened. Berg was also something of a sensualist and lets in a fair amount of lush late-Romantic tunefulness among the atonality, particularly in the interludes. The nightmarish bar-scene evocations of prole culture are effectively done.

WORDS

The execution of half-crazed murderer J.C. Woyzeck in Leipzig in 1824 was the basis of Georg Büchner's proto-Marxist play, left unfinished at his death from typhoid at the age of 23. The messy manuscript was deciphered in 1879 by Carl Franzos, who probably made some changes (including misreading the hero's name). Berg saw the play in 1914; the libretto is an abridged version.

PLOT

Act I *Put-upon soldier Wozzeck is teased mercilessly by his captain about his concubine and bastard child. Later he is beset by unpleasant visions. His girlfriend, Marie, casts admiring glances at the drum-major. Wozzeck is further mistreated by a doctor who pays him to experiment on him. The current experiment is to put Wozzeck on a 100% bean diet. We are not told what the results of this are, but Marie has sex with the drum-major.*

Act II *Wozzeck hands over his bean-money to Marie, and looks enquiringly at her new gold earrings. The captain and doctor make leaden jokes (they are Germans – whoops, Austrians – after all) about the drum-major and Marie, following which Wozzeck has an inconclusive row with her. That evening Wozzeck watches while Marie and the drum-major get into a clinch at a party. Afterwards, the drum-major beats Wozzeck up in the barracks dorm.*

Act III *Wozzeck takes Marie for a short walk and kills her. Then he goes to a bar and behaves oddly. He returns to the scene of the crime and manages to drown himself while trying to dispose of the murder weapon. Marie's death causes a small stir.*

CAUTIONARY NOTE

In 1920 Berg wrote an article entitled *The Musical Impotence of Hans Pfitzner*. Silly, really: Pfitzner (composer of *Palestrina* and other light classics) then naturally attempted to nobble Erich Kleiber, the conductor at the première of *Wozzeck*, and his acolytes tried with some success to disrupt the performance.

WHAT THE PAPERS SAID

"One must seriously ask oneself whether the practice of music can be criminal. In musical terms this is a capital offence." (*Deutsche Zeitung*)

CRUSH BAR GAMBIT

"Wozzeck's greatest innovation is arguably not musical but behavioural: he is the first operatic hero who, unburdened by crass notions of honour, elects to kill the guilty party, namely Marie, rather than the drum-major as all his aristocratic forebears would have done. At last a democratic concept of personal responsibility is born."

RECORDINGS

❖ Böhm, Fischer-Dieskau, Lear, Melchert, Berlin German Opera Chorus and Orchestra (DG) ❖ Dohnányi, Waechter, Silja, Winkler, Vienna State Opera Chorus, Vienna Philharmonic (Decca) ❖

Composers Index